Wisdom With
Understanding
is Better
Than Rubies

Lurine Karon Greenberg
Fine Arts Collection

WHAT SHE WANTS

WHAT SHE WANTS

Women Artists Look at Men

Edited by

NAOMI SALAMAN

With an Introduction by

LINDA WILLIAMS

VERSO

London · New York

farra

First published by Verso 1994
© Linda Williams, Naomi Salaman, Claire Pajaczkowska, Lola Young, Cherry Smyth 1994
Images © the artists
All rights reserved

Verso
UK: 6 Meard Street, London W1V 3HR
USA: 29 West 35th Street, New York, NY 10001-2291

Verso is the imprint of New Left Books

ISBN 0–86091–491–7
ISBN 0–86091–656–1 (pbk)

British Library Cataloguing in Publication Data
A catalogue record for this book is available from the British Library

Library of Congress Cataloging-in-Publication Data
A catalogue record for this book is available from the Library of Congress

Text design by Anna Del Nevo
Typeset by Solidus (Bristol) Limited
Printed and bound in Great Britain by
B.A.S. Printers, Over Wallop, Hampshire

CONTENTS

ACKNOWLEDGEMENTS

With thanks to Jane Williams.

What She Wants is an Impressions Gallery touring show funded by the Arts Council of Great Britain, curated by Naomi Salaman, assisted and produced by Impressions Gallery, York, and Orchard Gallery, Derry.

Part One

Ceci n'est pas un pénis.

INTRODUCTION:

WHAT DO I SEE? WHAT

DO I WANT?

Linda Williams

How shall I regard these sexual images of men made by women artists? Is this erotic art? Is this pornography? Is there a difference?

Distinctions between the erotic and the pornographic are often elusive, sometimes irrelevant and always political. Yet we seem willing to expend enormous amounts of time and energy in order to establish a firm line between the two. One reason it has become harder to draw a clear line between the erotic and the 'hard core' is that sexual identity has become politicized and 'speaking sex', representing 'sex', has become as necessary to gay, lesbian, sado-masochistic and other sexual activists as it has to those who would repress such speech.

My favourite example within the US sexual political scene of the necessity of speaking and showing sex even when the goal is to repress it goes to the heart of the question of spectatorship – of who gets to look and of how this 'look' is constructed – at issue in this volume. While running for re-election in 1990, conservative Senator Jesse Helms waved three portfolios of photographic nudes from Robert Mapplethorpe's 'Perfect Moment' exhibit on the floor of the Senate as examples of taxpayers' money being wasted on offensive smut. Helms invited the senators to examine the offending portfolios, but not before asking all the pages and 'all the ladies' to leave the room.[1] In attempting to point the finger at a 'bad' pornography, Helms had to bring the offending material on scene just as surely as any pornographer. But since part of his motive in banning such 'smut' was to protect young people and 'ladies' from such views, he could not allow them to see the very materials in question. He therefore rather comically attempted to reproduce the archaic exhibition conditions of the all-male smoker in which to show his 'smut'.

In a recent essay I tried to coin a term to describe this paradoxical situation of incessantly speaking and showing the sexual representations whose very propriety is at issue. The term is on/scenity.[2] If ob/scenity describes those sexual representations which a society agrees should remain off (ob) scene – just as men once decided that women could be the objects but not be the viewing subjects of sexually exciting 'dirty pictures' – then on/scenity describes the current situation of highly-contested, and much more diverse, sexual representations whose visibility is everywhere.

On/scenity seems to me to be a useful term because it points to the political importance of who controls sexual representation – who looks; who gets looked at; what gets constructed as sexually exciting – in an era of mass-media where the traditional ob/scenity of the gentlemen-only 'secret museum' is no longer fully in force. Although Jesse Helms tried hard to keep the women and pages from seeing Robert Mapplethorpe's photos, he had to show them to some sort of public in order to emphasize their obscenity. And, as we all know, the images he waved before this contested public were controversial precisely because they were not conventional, erotic images of women by straight men but sexually destabilizing eroto-pornographic images of naked and semi-naked black men and gay male sado-masochists.

There are good reasons to be suspicious of the vast amount of energy going into distinguishing between pornography and eroticism. Sometimes it seems to me that the only solution is to deny the value of any distinction whatsoever. At some level, pornography will always be the bad sexual representations that you like and eroticism the good, acceptable sexual representations that I like. However, this does not mean that some distinctions have not, historically at least, existed and that they do not powerfully influence the way we go about discussing this increasingly on/ scene body of work. Let me try to illuminate some of these distinctions, not in order to relegate a 'bad' pornography to the dustbin and promote a 'good' eroticism to museum-wall status, but in order to better appreciate why they are not so easily separable in the photos collected here.

Pornography aims frankly at arousal; it addresses the bodies of its observers in their sexual desires and pleasures. It boldly sells this sexual address to viewers as a commodity and it does not let aesthetic concerns or cultural prohibitions limit what it shows. Erotic art, on the other hand, is traditionally much less bold and (somewhat) less commercial. Because it is committed to the ideals of an art which is supposed to be beyond commodification and to reside within the rational limits of good taste, it does not directly (though it may indirectly) 'sell' its sexual address.

Yet, as Lynda Nead has shown in a recent essay, all erotic art, even the highest and most artistic, necessarily flirts with a degree of sexual address – if it didn't, it would simply become art. This contained flirtation with sexual taboos and outright physical arousal is crucial to the form. Here is how Nead describes it:

Erotic art legitimizes the representation of the sexual through the assertion of form which holds off the collapse into the pornographic. Erotic art takes the viewer to the frontier of legitimate culture; it allows the viewer to be aroused but within the purified, contemplative mode of high culture.[3]

In other words, erotic art 'flirts' with the sexual but ultimately reassures its spectators that the sexual can be formally and aesthetically contained. Similarly, I think, pornography needs to be viewed as carrying on its own flirtation with art, with the 'higher' regions of contemplation, before choosing to opt for the bold sexual address typical of this form. Thus a clear category of pornography may flirt with, but will ultimately abandon, the indirection of the erotic, while a clear category of erotic art may flirt with, but will ultimately abandon, the bold sexual address of the pornographic. So much for clear categories. It is theoretically impossible to separate the two categories, but the important point is that what is erotic will always depend on its tension with the pornographic and vice versa. Even more to the point, however, is the fact that the unorthodox sexuality will always seem, simply by virtue of its unorthodoxy, to offer the more bold sexual address, and thus will seem more pornographic than erotic.

Now, if we add to this, already muddy, distinction the added complication that the realistic effects of photography itself have often seemed to skew sexual images in the direction of the pornographic, then we begin to appreciate the full complexity of the issues facing this exhibit. For with the ability to capture the 'graphic' truths of the human body automatically, by simply pushing a button to register an indexical trace of objects in their actual time and place, theorists of both film and photography have viewed first the still and then the moving picture as inherently, 'ontologically', obscene.[4]

One of the earliest statements of photography's 'ontological obscenity' is by Charles Baudelaire who, in writing about the extreme realism of the photographic stereoscope, used it to denounce the whole of photography in this famous passage describing the Salon of 1859:

It was not long before thousands of pairs of greedy eyes were glued to the peephole of the stereoscope, as though they were the skylights of the infinite. The love of obscenity, which is as vigorous a growth in the heart of natural man as self-love, could not let slip such a glorious satisfaction.[5]

As Abigail Solomon-Godeau[6] and others have suggested, it is possible that Baudelaire's condemnation of the realistic medium of photography as inherently obscene was also a specific condemnation of the erotic content of the stereoscopes he viewed. Certainly, his description – of 'greedy' male eyes glued to the peephole, consuming images presumed to be female and finding, in that consumption, what appears to be an allusion to masturbatory satisfaction – is almost a caricature of contemporary notions of pornographic spectatorship as a visceral relation between the eyes consuming an indexical trace of the real body, bypassing the higher regions of contemplation.

Ever since Baudelaire, defenders of erotic photography have had to work overtime to carve out a space of aesthetically acceptable, non-obscene, 'good' erotic spectatorship. They have thus been especially reluctant to admit the element of bodily arousal and sexual desire that is always lurking in even the most 'tasteful' of erotic photographs. Yet, as Nead points out, some element of arousal and desire must be admitted, even if it is to be recontained by the erotic.

It once went without saying that the viewer in danger of being aroused in the scenarios described by both Nead and Baudelaire was male, just as it went without saying that the erotic-object-of-desire-in-danger-of-becoming-pornographic was female. Yet I think it is important to realize how often the real scandal lurking beneath the ostensible one of male 'greedy eyes', consuming images of woman, has been the possibility that some other 'greedy eyes' might be looking at sexually provocative images. If we read on, for example, in Baudelaire's denunciation of the obscenity of stereo-scopes we see that his horror at the idea of a woman looking through these peepholes is far greater than his first alarm at masculine 'greedy eyes':

I once heard a smart woman, a society woman, not of my society, say to her friends, who were discreetly trying to hide such pictures from her, thus taking it upon themselves to have some modesty on her behalf: 'Let me see: nothing shocks me.' That is what she said, I swear it, I heard it with my own ears; but who will believe me?[7]

Today, of course, the viewer in 'danger' of being pornographically aroused by erotic or pornographic images could be a heterosexual woman, a sadist, a masochist, a fetishist, a gay man, a lesbian, a bisexual, a heterosexual man or a combination. This may perhaps be the true scandal of contemporary on/scenity: the person who looks and who may be aroused may not be the 'natural man' to whom Baudelaire alludes in his first denunciation of photography. And what this person looks at and is potentially aroused by may not necessarily correspond to 'natural' affinities of race, class, gender or sexual orientation. The polymorphous perversity of on/scenity has altered the familiar relations of sexual difference and gendered viewing that once gave eroticism and pornography a certain stability. Under these altered conditions of on/scenity the line between the erotic and the pornographic becomes even less clear.

I raise these issues by way of introduction to the arresting photos in the 'What She Wants' exhibition because, though they are basic to any consideration of eroto-pornographic photography, they are especially important to this particular exhibition of photographs taken by women of men. The 'simple' fact that it is women viewers and women photographers who must negotiate this complicated tension, between the contemplative mode of high art and the arousal that is always a possibility in the representation of the sexual, changes everything. So too does the 'simple' fact that it is men who are the objects of this vision. This reversal is undeniably the crucial fact about this exhibit, and yet it does not change things in predictable ways.

The fact that my look at this exhibition of male bodies would scandalize both Charles Baudelaire and Jesse Helms encourages me to seek some broad generalizations about the difference of my look. However, I'm not sure of the difference my look at male bodies posed by and for women makes. Though it is certainly significant that women image-makers are negotiating the line between the erotic and the pornographic, and that male bodies are balancing on that line, this reversal alone may not lead to any startling liberations from the presumed objectifications of an all-controlling, and increasingly dubious, 'male gaze'.

W H A T   D O   I   S E E ?

I see a diverse group of photographs of men. Some of these I could classify as classically erotic: for example, Jacqueline Kennedy's image of a hip, thigh and partial fur of pubic area which 'tastefully' obscures the view of genitals (p. 93), or the black and white series by Chris Duyt of tightly-curled short hairs against unrecognizable swirls and folds of flesh (p. 145). Other images I could classify as pornographic: for example, again Jacqueline Kennedy's photo of 'other chambers', an apparently female hand inserted up to its bracelet in the rectum of a kneeling man (p. 138); or Yanna Papai-oannou's scrotum-to-neck view of a somewhat luridly-lit man holding the tip of his erect penis (p. 103). The examples of erotic images contain elements of the 'flirtation' with the directly sexual necessary to make them erotic and both of the examples of pornographic images contain flirtations with art: in 'other chambers' it is the bracelet and the light touch of the non-inserted hand; in the masturbation image it is the theatricality of the lighting.

It is fair to say, however, that the vast majority of these images cannot be easily classified as either clearly erotic or pornographic and that this blurring of the line is part of what they are most importantly about. Some of these images tend towards the playful and humorous – as in Tabitha Goode's game of locating the moist red tip of the penis among the red, moist strawberries, plums and cherries (p. 112), or Flo Fox's large penis hanging just over the edge of the window of a computer screen (p. 79). Does humour function here as the protective armour of a gender group that has had precious little practice placing either their 'greedy', or their flirtatious and contemplative, eyes at these particular peepholes? It may, but it is also worth noting that many of the more playful images slide easily from play into a more serious vein: as in Diane Baylis's strangely awesome 'land-scape' composed of reposing male body and sky (p. 71), or Naomi Salaman's pelvic X-ray with fleshy penis inserted against the ghostly bones (p. 130).

Certainly, men have had equally little practice opening up their bodies to a female 'look'. One of the few male subjects to gaze back confidently at the camera appears in Sara Leigh Lewis's portrait of a muscular, bearded man, arms over his head, who eyes the camera with sexual assurance. More often, however, we don't see the man's head, or if we do, he does not gaze back at the camera. Indeed, there is a marked fascination with the body part. Yet the attraction to parts over wholes is not a distant objectification. Can we say it is the gender of the photographer that chooses so many vulnerable, fragile, soft or slender bodies? Is it the gender of Lucinda Beatty that chooses to pose a delicate male torso floating in water with a veil on top (p. 95)? I don't know.

Nor do I know if it is the gender of the photographer that determines the frequent relations of intimacy that seem to obtain between picture-taker and subject, as in Iona Fabian's disarming photo of a smiling bearded man holding his crotch, with his pants down (p. 80). If so, however, this intimacy does not preclude the introduction of elements of power, as in Yanna Papaioannou's view of a naked foot (could it be the photographer's?) pressing against a vulnerable soft and reddish penis (p. 110). While the pose might seem debasing, everything else in the image – warm colours, rosy wet penis, soft pressing of foot – contributes to a contradictory closeness and warmth.

Very few images suggest that staple of erotic-pornographic imagery: the voyeur looking in on a private scene. One example, however, is Shanta Rao's arresting photo of the side view of a man looking down at his erect penis in his hand glimpsed through a thin gap in some curtains (p. 100). On the other hand, there are a great variety of photos that might be seen to fetishize the male organ. Some of the most beautiful and striking of these are: Hermione Wiltshire's calm image of a floating, porcelain penis upon which two delicate butterflies pose (p. 136); Robin Shaw's black-and-white close-up of the veins, hairs and bumps of a penis (p. 128); Ruth Rubine's elegant black-and-white portrait of a gloved, handcuffed hand grasping an erect penis, also handcuffed, at its base (p. 140). In this photo the violence of the handcuff and erection is tempered by the odd propriety of the glove. In another by Herlinda Koelbl the delicate curve of a soft uncircumcised penis is accented by the equally delicate head of a cockerel (p. 127).

Does the presence of so many penises attest to some sort of homage to the phallus? It seems likely that these hard and soft penises are far too individual to represent the phallic, law-of-the-father so familiar to feminist theorizing. These penises, even the more dressed-up and glamorous of them, are somehow too distinct to stand in for more than what they are: variable mounds of flesh in various states of arousal and repose, sometimes dressed up, sometimes plain. Perhaps the reason for all this rather friendly curiosity lies not in the supposed lack-in-being for which the phallus serves as substitute in Lacanian theory but in the much more mundane fact that these highly various mounds of flesh constitute a very new subject area for women photographers. There is a process of discovery at work here and just a little fascination with an object that, in so many other places, has, for women observers at least, been the last taboo.

I do not mention the above groupings, and tentative generalizations, because I think images of intimacy are preferable to voyeurism, nor do I mention them to bemoan the fact that women artists show as great – although of a different kind – a fascination with the penis as does hard-core pornography by men. I don't know what these generalizations say about the gender reversal that is the premiss of this exhibit. I do know, however, that it is important not to contrast these sexual images of men by women too rigidly with stereotypes of sexual images of women by men. I don't know what to make, for example, of Sophie Molins's side view of a penis pissing in a sink, the stream of urine cutting through a shaft of sunlight (p. 121). I know that I recognize it as a familiar gesture of every man I have ever known and perhaps a gesture whose simplicity I envy. Is this all that penis envy is?

In short, I do not think I can generalize in any useful way about the images collected here. The remarkable feat of these photographs is to have undertaken this gender role reversal without falling back on the easy smirk of turning tables on pornography or, perhaps even more importantly, without resorting to an overly safe containment of the bold pornographic sex that sells by a highly aestheticized eroticism. The photos we see in this book are raunchy, beautiful, funny, awesome and tender. They ask me to look anew at bodies and organs I know well but which I have rarely seen pictured for me. So what do I see? I see pornography and eroticism, I see intimacy and distance, I see penises and phalluses. What do I want? Most of all, I want the chance to keep exercising my greedy eyes, the chance to keep looking.

September 1993
Irvine, California

NOTES

1. Edward de Grazia, *Girls Lean Back Everywhere: The Law of Obscenity and the Assault on Genius*, Random House, New York 1992, p. 637.

2. Linda Williams, 'Pornographies On/Scene, or "diff'rent strokes for diff'rent folks"', in Lynne Segal and Mary McIntosh (eds), *Sex Exposed: Sexuality and the Pornography Debate*, Virago, London 1992.

3. Lynda Nead, '"Above the pulp-line": The Cultural Significance of Erotic Art', in Pamela Church Gibson and Roma Gibson (eds), *Dirty Looks: Women, Pornography, Power*, British Film Institute, London 1993, p. 147.

4. Stanley Cavell writes, for example: 'the ontological conditions of the cinema reveal it as inherently pornographic' (Stanely Cavell, *The World Viewed*, Harvard University Press, Cambridge, Mass. 1979, p. 45). Fredric Jameson states that 'pornographic films are . . . only the potentiation of film in general, which ask us to stare at the world as though it were a naked body' (Fredric Jameson, *Signatures of the Visible*, Routledge, New York 1990, p. 1).

5. Charles Baudelaire, 'The Modern Public and Photography' in Alan Trachtenberg, ed., *Classic Essays on Photography*, Leete's Island Books, New Haven, Conn. 1980, pp. 83–9.

6. Abigail Solomon-Godeau, 'Reconsidering Erotic Photography: Notes for a Project of Historical Salvage', in *Photography at the Dock: Essays on Photographic History, Institutions, and Practices*, University of Minnesota Press, Minneapolis 1991.

7. Charles Baudelaire, 'The Modern Public'.

REGARDING MALE OBJECTS

Naomi Salaman

In my research for 'What She Wants' I have considered the absence of a history of erotic representations of the male nude by the female artist. I have come across complex cultural resistances to the practice of looking at and representing the man's sex. Here I want to consider this problematic of taboo and exclusion by asking two questions: 'Why have there been no great women pornographers?', and 'What does she see when she looks?'

The first is a rhetorical question to invoke the initial feminist question in art history, 'Why have there been no great women artists?'[1] Linda Nochlin's essay from 1973 sets out a critical enquiry into the institutions which make up art, history and gender, questioning the narratives of cultural value and genius on which the status of art rests. By adding 'pornography' to the original question about great women artists I hope to invoke these materialist questions about relative cultural value, and to add to them the question of visual pleasure and bodily arousal. Pornography is about the autoerotic – how looking at certain images can spark the body off; it is an aesthetics of interlocking bodily sensations, both visual and sexual. Different images affect different viewers, and of course it is not only pornography which is based on autoeroticism. None the less the 'bad' meaning of pornography is its improper effect on the body. Pornography, unlike art, is not considered in terms of 'greatness'; in fact there are few available means of evaluating it. We may be able to find a content analysis, but more than that – what it does aesthetically, qualifying how it makes you feel, unless it is righteous feminist anger or religious indignation – is not much documented, except as social science data. In general, pornography tends to be considered along with everything else regrettable in modern society – it's cheap, nasty, tacky, tasteless, vile, repetitive, inhuman, exploitative, crime-infested. Pornographers, unlike other photographers and film-makers, are not celebrated as artists and are not generally known by name. On the other hand porn stars, like film stars, are. This is where Madonna fell between terms – asking, as she did, to be considered an artist for producing the book *Sex*.[2] The closest she would get to being recognized as a visual artist would be to be known as a great artist's model. Steve Meisel will always be seen as the eye behind those striking images.

Other confusions frequently occur between the two different value systems of pornography and art. When the Mapplethorpe retrospective was shut down in Cincinatti, Ohio, in 1988, and the organizers put on trial for exhibiting pornography, it was the art historians' presentation of Mapplethorpe's work in terms of composition, chiaroscuro and timeless traditions of figure and ground that convinced the jury and saved the curator from criminal prosecution.

The artist Jeff Koons has worked on this recently with his 'Made in Heaven' series: large colour photo tableaux of himself and his porn star, ex-wife, La Cicciolina engaged in sexual acts.[3] Koons was in no danger of not being recognized as an artist by appearing himself in the image, as he is already well established; the series 'Made in Heaven' is shown in international art galleries, and costs $100,000 a piece. Cicciolina's status, on the other hand, was much diminished; she was not even credited as a collaborator.[4]

Only ex-porn star Annie Sprinkle has addressed this division head-on by becoming a 'Post-Porn Modernist' performance artist. Now she makes art films and does art performances about her life and loves as a sex worker.

Any attempt to unravel the lack of erotic images of men by women artists will have to take into account the public contempt for pornography and its associated activity of masturbation, alongside the virtuous achievement associated with art masterpieces.

The two cultural practices of art and pornography differ in how they are measured, but overlap in other important ways as their central theme has been rendering the human figure, and they have shared figurative conventions, studio models, technologies and technicians. They also overlap as sites of production of images and points of view which are traditionally all male. In order for there to have been great women pornographers there would have to have been great women artists. To argue that there have been no great women pornographers is to forget the creative and energetic work of women porn stars, but to include them is to be blind to the gender tradition of high art, and the convention of the male gaze which has structured the narratives and sexuality of western visual culture.

Before a pornography/erotica which implicates women looking at men is considered, the traditional overlaps in art history and pornography of women **not** looking at men have to be thought through.

From the Enlightenment on, the art academies of Europe and America placed great intellectual emphasis on the study of the male nude. Within the classical ideal the male body was the perfectly proportioned architectural form and the life room was a place of great learning where only the most accomplished students and academicians could enter. Women artists were not permitted.

In the heyday of history painting women faced manifest institutional obstacles to becoming successful artists, as the route to recognition was via the life room, from which they were barred.[5] It is ironic that their figurative and career ambitions should have focused this way on the body of the naked man. The male figure is almost overburdened by proscription before women artists even got a glance at him – let alone a leer.

In France, as elsewhere in the 1890s, the issue of allowing women into the academy was hotly debated, particularly the idea of women in the life room. Those against argued that women lacked the abstract mental power needed for the work and worried about the modesty of the women, the possibility that the male model may become aroused, as well as the usual fear of competition and threat of depopulation that may ensue with the advent of professional women. By the time the progressive educationalists won the arguments, at the end of the century, and women were admitted to separate classes to study from a partly clothed model, the prestige of history painting was over and academic life drawing skills were no longer such a prerequisite for an artist's career.

With a few notable exceptions, the history of representing the male nude within the western tradition is a history of men representing men. What is interesting here is not so much a missing history of women artists, but rather that implicit in the history of the classic male nude is the practice of excluding women as artists. Women have been allowed to admire works of art – including the male nude – in galleries, but women artists were severely restricted from becoming part of the high cultural process of representing the male form. While the history of the life class offers a narrative of anxiety about women looking at men, this is only one side of this story. We can hardly surmise what the women artist sees when she is not allowed to look.

In 'Beautiful Bodies and Dying Heroes',[6] Alex Potts writes about the male nude in the paintings of David during the French revolutionary period around 1799. He argues that David's pictorial strategy and his declared revolutionary intent involved a new rendering of the heroic male figures. These grand paintings were state messages to the people, intended to inspire the Republic. Whether it be the winning warrior of 'The Intervention of the Sabines', or the single dead youth of 'The Death of Joseph Bara', Potts describes the formal beauty of the male figure as the 'primary signifier of heroic virtue',[7] over and above traits of character. 'It was only in the representation of an ideally beautiful male body that tensions between body as the sign of pleasure and desire, and an ethical investment of the body as the sign of an ideal subjectivity, the ideal subjectivity of the virtuous and "free" republican subject could be played out.'[8] This 'free' virtuous republican is, of course, assumed to be a man: 'The beautiful male figure can thus function as an ideal object of desire and as an ideal subjectivity with which the male spectator can identify.'[9] This combination is indeed a powerful lure for those it addresses. This highly charged practice of figuration is a process of the state asking its young fit male citizens to join the revolutionary army. In return they are fitted with ideal subjectivity – otherwise known as a uniform. And how exquisite is the ideal male hero almost already lost in battle.

Alex Potts identifies a particular emergence of the erotic male nude within changing social cultural and aesthetic conditions. Can we begin to articulate how these images were seen by women at the time? It is difficult to backdate a reading of an image without assuming an ahistorical observer and in this case a universal woman viewer, and I want to avoid any such generalizations. Potts outlines the way in which David's paintings may address the male subject on two levels of identification; both being an ideal citizen, modelled on the elevated public values of ancient Greece, and having an ideal form, modelled on a perfectly proportioned, young athletic male body. Perhaps it is possible to conjecture these two modes of identification in terms of the female spectator. If David's central male figures were images of ideal subjects of an ideal republic, then men, women, old and young could participate in a joint patriotic identification with them. (That is not to say that they all did.) Although it is the male body here which is idealized, the transsexual nature of the women's identification would not be much out of place alongside other trans-generational ones. Here we have identification with an ego ideal: it does not have to resemble us in any way. However, the other level of identification that Potts mentions is a narcissistic one, that these beautiful bodies are the 'ideal objects of desire', an ideal ego, which offers the male viewer a form of infantile regression, infinitely erotic, 'free' from troubling attachments to other objects. For the female observer these beautiful painted bodies may tantalize but they will only be ideal egos if the woman wants to dress up as a boy soldier. Otherwise these figures represent the state's actual claim to the real bodies of the men around her – brothers, sons, fathers, lovers. Perhaps she is prepared to let them go, again for 'la Patrie', or maybe she knows that she has no choice and just fears for their lives. The difference here is in the modality of looking – the difference between an economy of desire; the narcissism of the soldier being 'called' up, and an economy of love; the loss felt watching them go.

Perhaps this could be taken one stage further. The male body becomes the property of the state in times of war, and representations of the ideal male body traditionally signify national security or national pride. The inverse of this is found in contemporary gay culture, where there is a rich tradition of cabaret acts and chorus lines of athletes, soldiers and sailors. Here a parade of intense erotic figuration can interweave layers of disobedience and transgression − subjects and objects of an ideal erotic body that runs amok over the law of the father. They can dress up as real men and do the one thing that real men are not supposed to do. Yet when the same cabaret opens for a modern-day hen night, the dynamic of desire and transgression seem utterly consumed by something else − comedy. And beyond the comedy, the literal reversal of women stripping for men, there is a parade of men in uniform, or cowboys shooting each other, or ancient Greek gods with massive pillars. The camp humour is muffled, here we have men being 'men', which as we know is being 'ideal' occluding the being female. If such male entertainment acts for women as the Chippendales provoke laughter, it may be laughter which relieves anxiety otherwise associated with grief and depression.

The question of what she sees, then, in relation to this heroic/erotic male nude, is not just a matter of what she is allowed to see, what her status is, what her rights are, but also how the discourse of the male nude addresses her subjectivity, her sexuality.

In 'Techniques of the Observer',[10] Jonathan Crary discusses vision as a historical process of how the eye and the body have been articulated within the changing definitions of the individual. His argument is that the perceptual philosophy of the late eighteenth and early nineteenth centuries radically altered the dominant model of vision, on which a model of knowledge, individual thought and subjectivity rested. The camera obscura was the classic optical metaphor from the Enlightenment onwards, used by Descartes and later by Newton to illustrate the properties of light and to represent individual vision. The subject had 'sight' in the same way that light passed through a hole into a darkened room and inverted images of reality project on a screen. It was not until early studies in perception began to concentrate on the physical body of the observer that this model was questioned, calling up what Crary calls the 'carnal density of vision'. The eye of the classical observer, like the camera obscura, had one fixed point through which a single instantaneous reflection of the world was imported. We have two eyes, two different images of reality, neither more accurate than the other. Unlike the camera obscura our vision is temporary, prone to fatigue and lags slightly in time. The neutral medium of air through which light travels in a camera obscura is for the embodied eye a non-transparent opacity of blood and flesh, in which we produce phenomena not immediately tied to the external world: after-images and visions.

Crary identifies a 'modernization of vision' with a period between 1820 and 1840; a time when certain 'philosophical visual toys' exploded into mass production. Through the moving slots of a phenakistiscope, for instance, single images of a horse appeared as a horse in motion. These and other such toys were being sold as popular entertainment, exploiting the newly questioned mechanisms of perception and uprooting the idea of vision being linked to a stable external reality. The emergence of a modernized observer, Crary argues, impacted on the boundaries and definitions of the individual by rupturing the metaphor of the camera obscura and the transparence of vision and putting in its place a darker, opaque one, in which the observer's reality was no longer tied to objective truth.

What Crary does not touch on is the question of the conditions of the emergence of a female observer. We know that the individuated man of reason, the classical Cartesian subject, is an ideal and does not inhabit the flesh. None the less we somehow know him to be 'not female'. The modernized observer, the corporealized observer as Crary has it, is in a body, although one which is not clearly sexed. Bodies are perhaps not as clearly sexed from the inside as they are gendered by outside regulations. We can say that images are felt by the body but what relation does this bodily sensation of vision have to the discourse of female subjectivity, which in Crary's terms enables visual phenomena to come into view? Women and men can see clearly using the decorporealized universal Cartesian model of optics, but at the same time modern subjectivities, universal suffrage and women's rights have affected vision. The question is, what models of subjectivity are evoked by modern feminisms? Can we trace the emergence of a female observer? And if so, what models of sexual difference and pleasure would be implied?

Although it is not within the scope of this chapter to analyse the multitude of modern-day feminisms, there are two examples I would like to draw on. The first relates to the mass-media feminism of current anti-pornography campaigns, and the second to the critical post-modern feminism developed by Griselda Pollock and Rozika Parker.[11]

It is noticeable that the anti-pornography arguments based on radical feminist writer Andrea Dworkin make particular assumptions about vision:

We believe that pornography relentlessly communicates one message and one message only; this is what women are, this is what women want, this is how women deserve to be treated – i.e. with contempt, humiliation and as apparent willing victims of exploitation and violence. We believe therefore that pornography is propaganda against women which perpetuates sexism, sex discrimination and sexual violence.[12]

To insist that 'pornography communicates one message and one message only' is to put in place a classic model of vision and knowledge in which the viewer sees the world objectively from a single unchanging viewpoint. The meaning of the images are timeless, their effects are transparent and verifiable. This classic model of vision is here linked to a literal model of communication where the depiction of violence is considered the same as actual violence. In this definition of pornography there is a coherent message in the text and a passive male viewer; pornography has one meaning and one viewpoint and it is male – the female subject cannot be but a victim of his action. While the pressure groups lobbying against pornography now run professional media campaigns, adopting a post-modern approach to popular culture and reaching a mass audience, their basic arguments about the image and meaning imply a thoroughly pre-modern observer.

In *Old Mistresses*, Griselda Pollock and Rozika Parker consider a reversal of the relations of looking and being looked at in terms of the female nude: 'A man can be placed in a feminine position but will not become feminine. Because of the social power of men in our society no man can ever be reduced to a crumpled heap of male flesh in the dark corner of some women's studio.'[13] The reasons they outline as to why a woman artist may attempt such a reversal are aimed at deconstructing the supposed natural femininity of dominant representations of the female nude. This will not work, they argue, because men will always be men, no matter how they are represented, no matter who is looking at them. Here Pollock and Parker also adopt a rigid classical position where men cannot be imagined without their power. *Old Mistresses* describes the project of feminist art as a strategic questioning of femininity and representation. It uses an analysis of sexual difference as a social/psychic system of meaning based in language and representation, and as such has laid out the ground of much critical work.

Evaluating art work in terms of 'Textual Strategies',[14] i.e. that art either works to deconstruct certain ideology or it does not work, has been an influential aspect of critical post-modernism. The drawback is that some of the more ambiguous intentions of visual practice, and some of the more insolent pleasures of production, have been dismissed as 'art for art's sake'; a deeply unsatisfactory motivation for contemporary political artists and theorists. Yet as Crary has indicated, it is precisely developments in visual play and visual pleasure which added to the theory of vision and have had a significant role in the emergence of a modernized observer.

In conclusion, I would like to consider the two questions raised here – 'Why have there been no great women pornographers?', and 'What does she see when she looks?' – by asking a third question, 'What does she see when she looks at a penis?'

'Sammy' by Kay Hart (page 131) is a toned photograph of a close-haired dog on its back legs, taken from behind. At first glance the cropped figure resembles the naked torso of a beast/man; well-defined muscles, big thighs and a large solid penis. It is the back of a dog in which we see the front of a man. The references of resemblance, on which this image tilts back and forth between handsome hound and phallic man, are seductive. We think we are looking at the crotch of a man even though we know we are looking at a dog. This is the logic of metaphor, the dog stands in the place of something else; it can signify both through its fur and tail, as well as through its likeness to a male torso.

Penis envy, it has been argued, is not envy of an actual penis but rather a wish for an idealized penis.[15] Does this mean that 'Sammy' could be seen as a representation of penis envy? This question opens out the problematic of desire and representation, twin terms which cannot be separated but which cannot really illuminate each other either. The wish for an idealized penis is a wish to represent phallic sexuality, which the little girl is rigorously discouraged from. But this wish to have a phallus, or to represent autoeroticism, does not necessarily translate into a desire to look at the penis – quite the reverse in fact, because the penis becomes the reason for her unhappiness. While Sammy can represent a phallus and not a penis, this image is not about penis envy in the classical Freudian sense, firstly because here is an image about wanting to look, not about *not wanting to look*, and secondly because once a wish becomes consciously articulated it ceases to be part of an unconscious process and becomes something else. Instead I would call 'Sammy' a penis fantasy; one which is narcissistic and nostalgic in mode. Here we have a tail/penis as metaphor for uninhibited phallic sexuality – a reinvention of what every child once was – 'cocky', full of himself, made of a solid consistency like chocolate, a smooth firm surface, like Sammy, like an everlasting erection. There is no interior body here, no mess, just firm hard shape and surface. Nothing can get to Sammy; even a chopped-off tail has *grown back* to a gleaming picture of perfect proportions.

In 'Sink' by Sophie Molins (page 121), a man is pissing in a bathroom sink. The sink is pale milky porcelain, its form and volume highlighted by a shaft of light coming from the left. One tap is plumbed in, next to it are two holes. Underneath is a waste trap and a strong angular shadow. On the right is a dark figure leaning on the edge of the sink. The top of his thigh has a pale highlight along its edge delineating it from the sink which echoes the body-like form and tone. The man's penis points into the bowl and down. Underneath the shadow of the waste points along and up. Into the sink urine spurts out in an arch, under which two shadows are drawn onto the lustre surface of the curved sink bowl.

The composition and tonal qualities of this image present us with a range of equivalences between the elements. The penis and the tap, both with nozzle, both for passing water, both dripping or flowing depending on pressure. The penis and the waste trap, both solid cylindrical forms, which hang down from a round bowl/body. The penis head and the porcelain moulding, both curvaceous, taut and seamless. The sculptural ridges and rims of the inverted relief of the soap dish visually double the intricate but smooth moulding where the head of the penis joins the stem.

These relationships between form and function, porcelain and skin, moulding and erection are temporary, held by the moment of this photograph. To ask if this image is phallic would not lead immediately to the penis so much as to a list of evocations: the penis, the glistening piss, the sink rim, the waste trap. A chain of references that are unstable; the piss will come to an end, the light will move, the semi-hard penis will go soft. Here there is no one metaphor to stand in for 'it', as with 'Sammy'. Instead there are momentary connections between things, words and bodies, and with that an intimacy of fleeting physical reverberations.

The question 'what does she see when she looks at a penis', sets up for the female observer a variety of modes in which to view the image of the male body, in relation to her body, her vision and her desire. The 'What She Wants' project began as an enquiry into the absence of erotic images of men made by women and set up an 'experimental reversal' of traditions. It soon became evident that reversal is a far from adequate term to describe the process of women looking at men, as there is no symmetry in the construction of sexual difference, nor in the history of the male and female nude. Rather, this reversal initiates a transformation that soon loses contact with the original format. When women artists attempt to represent men as the beautiful object they will not effect a social reversal of power, but they can affect the scopic regimes, and this can translate into new knowledge, new 'abstract power' in the debates of pleasure and representation. It is not a case of representing men the way men have represented women, but rather one of constructing links and finding echoes within the discourse of the male nude, masculinity and representation. The fantasies located around 'Sammy'; wanting to display/investigate, embody/incorporate the metaphorical phallus, and the equivalences and slippages of an intimate moment in 'Sink' that move between the visual and the verbal, are just two examples. They both begin to articulate ways in which a modernized female observer can look at the male body and play with the legacies of his vision without having to occlude her desiring body and its variety of identifications.

I would like to thank Clare Bayley, Sarah Pucill, Olivier Richon and Martha Kapos for their comments and suggestions.

NOTES

1. Linda Nochlin, 'Why have there been no great women artists?', in Thomas B. Hess, *Art and Sexual Politics*, Collier Books, New York 1973.
2. Madonna, *Sex*, Martin Secker & Warburg, London 1992.
3. Strikingly, this series has apparently had no problems with the censors, which is remarkable as the images contain graphic depictions of sexual acts which are not permitted to be shown in hard-core pornography in this country, such as penetration, anal penetration and ejaculation.
4. La Cicciolina is a porn star and one-time Italian politician. Jan Avkigos gave a talk at the Art Historians' Conference, London 1993 in which she showed clips from Cicciolina's videos alongside Koon's recent work. Much of the *mise-en-scène* and many of the motifs of her work are literally transposed.
5. See, for instance, Nikolaus Pevsner, *Academies of Art, Past and Present*, Cambridge University Press, Cambridge 1940, and more recently Tamar Garb, 'The Forbidden Gaze', in Kathleen Adler and Marcia Pointon (eds), *The Body Imaged*, Cambridge University Press, Cambridge 1993.
6. Alex Potts, 'Beautiful Bodies and Dying Heroes' *History Workshop Journal* no. 30, Autumn 1990.
7. Ibid., p. 3.
8. Ibid., p. 8.
9. Ibid., p. 11.
10. Jonathan Crary, *Techniques of the Observer: on Vision and Modernity in the Nineteenth Century*, MIT Press, Cambridge, Mass. 1990.

11. Griselda Pollock and Rozika Parker, *Old Mistresses: Women, Art and Ideology*, Routledge & Kegan Paul, London 1981.

12. The Campaign Against Pornography and Censorship, Policy Statement 1989.

13. Pollock and Parker, p. 124.

14. Judith Barry and Sandy Flitterman, 'Textual Strategies: the politics of art making', *Screen*, vol. 21, no. 2, 1980.

15. Maria Torok, 'The Meaning of "Penis Envy" in Women', 1963, in *Differences, A Journal of Feminist Cultural Studies*, vol. 4, spring 1992, special issue on 'The Phallus'.

THE PENIS AND THE PHALLUS

Claire Pajaczkowska

When is a penis not a penis?
When it's a phallus

A penis is a phallus whenever it is represented, thought of, imagined, desired, or fantasized about. Whenever it is something other than its biological self: the multi-purpose organ of masculine micturition, sexuality and reproduction. Since human sexuality can be separated from reproduction, and since sexuality becomes one of the structures of identity and intrasubjective consciousness, as well as one potential dynamic of inter-subjective relationships, the multi-purpose organ is inseparable from its representation.

Moreover, the phallus may be something that seems completely unconnected with penises or sexuality at all; to quote the example that amazed Freud[1] a 'shine on the nose' may turn out to be a 'glance at the nose', with the desire to look being displaced from activity to passivity and from below to above. The phallus is a signifier, and its materiality may turn out to be as imaginary as the signified it connotes. The phallus is very much linked to visibility and to the reversible logic of symmetry of the imaginary, hence the possible substitution of 'shine' and 'glance'. Something that is seen can represent something that sees, passive can be transformed into active, absence can become presence, in the logic of the imaginary. We shall explore why it is that such fantasies of inversion are so closely linked to the structure of visual perception, and why it is that they are such a comforting substitute for acknowledgement of the fact of difference.

WHAT IS A SIGNIFIER?

It was through the conceptual revolution of structuralism that western culture finally realized the significance of language, and other forms of symbolism, in human subjectivity. Before this the limits of language had become the limits of philosophy, or as Wittgenstein put it 'Of what we cannot speak we must remain silent'. Other humanities and arts subjects had begun to explore the legacy of formalism, such as the Russian formalism of literary analysis, formalist linguistics, conceptual and material formalism in art. Structuralism, with its intellectual tributaries originating from sources in Marx, Saussure and Freud (to cite only those identified by Claude Lévi-Strauss), provided a basis for expanding the insights of formalism and making real, interdisciplinary, connections between a range of theories. It was Jacques Lacan who first proposed a systematic exploration of psychology from the perspective of structuralist linguistics; and it was he who suggested that subjectivity was a form of 'virtual reality' created by the technology of language. This proved to be antithetical to the basic principles of humanism and was intended as a critique of what Lacan called 'ego psychology'.

Some feminists have found that the work of Lacan illuminates the obscurity of the gender conundrum. The metaphor of casting light on darkness in order to render the unknown visible is a metaphor that is characteristic of Freud and Lacan in their approach to the 'dark continent' of female sexuality, and is derived from the same Enlightenment philosophy that differentiates between the rational and the irrational as a ratio of one to the other. If modernity has brought about post-Enlightenment transformations of this logic of rationality it has done so through the work of Freud, whose inspired exploration of the 'id' and the 'unconscious' cannot but surpass his own dictum that the whole purpose of psychoanalysis is to colonize the territory of the unconscious for conscious mastery: 'Where id was, there ego shall be.'

Of all the modern theories which require a transformation of rationality, the theories grouped under the general term structuralism have been the most powerful since the impact of psychoanalysis on the twentieth-century intellect. Structuralism undermines the rational differentiation between nature and culture, the basis of the differentiation between body and representation, between penis and phallus. It suggests that nature is always mediated by culture, and that the need to conceptualize in terms of binary oppositions is inherent in the innate structures of language. Our capacity for language and signification is both biological, 'natural' and social, 'cultural'. Structuralists such as anthropologist Claude Lévi-Strauss point out that humans are naturally social. Psychoanalysts such as John Bowlby and Donald Winnicott suggest that with the human mammalian heritage of extended infantile dependency, natural sociability has become a psychical fact, and not only a social and biological fact.

The fact of extended infantile dependency is cited by Freud as being the *sine qua non* of psychic development. It is, later, reinterpreted by post-Freudian 'object relations' psychoanalysis as being the most central influence on our adult subjectivity. We shall explore the differences between Freudian and post-Freudian psychoanalysis later, but I shall first describe the meaning of the theory of 'phallic monism', and the application of this theory to accounts of visual representation.

It was Freud who first suggested a theory of 'phallic monism', the idea that in the adult unconscious is the residual, unshakeable belief of the pre-oedipal child that all beings are endowed with a phallus. The popularity of Babar provides a glimmer of recognition of this fantasy, the world of anthropomorphic elephants ruled by a king and queen, with lots of little elephants, who are all united by bearing the trophy of their royalty, the beautiful, visible, facial trunk.

According to Freud, there is no difference between the libidinal structure of little girls and little boys when it comes to the phallic phase of development: both are unaware of the reality of the difference between male and female, just as they are unable to understand the difference between adult and child. Lacan's work has traced the level at which adult unconscious fantasy recapitulates this stage of development, showing that many aspects of 'normal' adult thought are, in fact, regressive fantasy. According to Freudian developmental theory the phallic phase precedes the resolution of the Oedipal drama in the 'beneficial tragedy' of the castration complex. For some, this term is an unnecessarily obtuse name for the process through which children enter into self-consciousness and educability, the first 'primal repression' separating the spheres of 'psychical' reality and 'material' reality as a precursor to the process of repression which will structure adult consciousness. Where the castration complex cannot be accepted and resolved, through too much anxiety, insecurity or other forms of deprivation, there will be a tendency to regress to previous states of consciousness as a defence against the dread of loss. This is when the phallic phase, and its characteristic fantasies, can be resurrected and embellished as a defence against reality and change.

FETISHISM

One of the characteristic fantasies of a phallic defence, against anxiety about loss of infantile omnipotence and acceptance of external reality, is the fetish. Although it has specific meanings in anthropology and in Marxist theory, in psychoanalytic terms fetishism is an expression of an unconscious fantasy that woman is endowed with a phallus. According to Freud the fantasy can take the form of one of two main images: either the woman is represented as having some externally visible phallic attribute, or else she is secretly believed to have 'stolen' and kept the male phallus inside herself. According to Ruth Mac Brunswick this fantasy arises

to insure the mother's possession of the penis and as such probably arises at the moment when the child becomes uncertain that the mother does indeed possess it.

Previously it seemed more than probable that the executive organ of the active mother is the breast; the idea of the penis is projected back upon the active mother after the importance of the phallus has been recognised.[2]

It is of significance here that the fetish has the structure of an image, albeit an imaginary image or fantasy. The phallic phase is closely linked to the importance of sight – indeed, Winnicott calls it the phase of 'swank and swagger'. What this means is that the fear of the loss of difference is articulated around a moment of vision, and also that the means by which the 'missing' signifier of difference is resurrected is through the image.

The second aspect that concerns us here is that this drama of difference is played out simultaneously across generations and across genders. It is a child who would rather not know the difference between itself and its parent, for fear of experiencing the devastatingly humiliating recognition of its own smallness and helplessness. It is a child who would rather not know the fact of sexual difference, another loss of the infantile omnipotence which allowed it the fantasy of being everything, everywhere, all the time.

This fusion of the denial of the difference between the generations and the difference between the sexes forms the basis for fetishism, and this Freudian view is different from Lacan's account. For Lacanians sexual difference is a law unto itself, linked to the fact of the binary oppositions structured into language and thus into human thinking. But for Freudians this logic of phallic monism is the infantile logic that is specific to one developmental phase, an archeological fact rather than an actual fact.

The idea of the 'phallic woman' therefore serves as a counter-idea to the idea of woman as castrated, lacking or damaged, each fantasy reflecting the other in a dyad of defence. The insecurity of such a fantasy means that it must constantly be substantiated by 'proof', and in the case of the phallic phase 'proof' is usually sought in visibility. Images are then generated, or found, which confirm this idea of the phallic woman or its counterpart, the idea of the castrated woman.

As Freud has suggested, the phallus attributed to the woman is a substitute for the missing maternal phallus which the fetishist disavows.

And, as Ruth Mac Brunswick has suggested, the phallus may be an imaginary penis which is retrospectively projected onto 'the executive organ of the active mother': the breast. Here the pre-oedipal stage is recognized as being central to the structure of the logic of phallic monism. The phallus as signifier of difference is all the more urgently needed in order to protect the child from the threat of passive dependency on the active mother.

There are certain forms of visual representation which reanimate this fantasy and which are based on a structure of fetishism. Some forms of art obsessively depict the female nude in such a way that the very repetition of the theme expresses the depth of the anxiety that woman's body generates for our culture. One example is the graphics and paintings of Allen Jones, described by Laura Mulvey, in a pioneering essay for *Spare Rib*, as fetishistic defences against the comprehension of sexual difference. Mulvey went on to elaborate her theory in relation to cinema, extending the understanding of fetishism as figurative image to include within the definition the spectator's relation to the structure of the gaze. The oscillation between disbelief ('it's only a picture'), and the suspension of disbelief (the illusion necessary to culture), is itself a replication of the psychic structure of fetishism which oscillates between acknowledgement and disavowal of the reality of difference.[3] French film theorist Christian Metz also proposed a Freudian reading of the dynamics of cinema spectatorship, which came to a similar conclusion about the centrality of the mechanism of fetishism in visual representation. However, further to this, Mulvey explores the relation between narrative and spectatorship in cinema, showing that classic realism depends on a hierarchy of active and passive identifications in which activity is associated with masculinity and control, while passivity is associated with femininity and objectification.[4] Whereas this narrative 'control' is the expression of an unconscious fantasy of sadism linking voyeurism to the ability to 'make something happen', objectification expresses the complementary fantasy of masochistic exhibitionism and waiting for something 'to be done'. That the former is associated with masculinity and the latter with femininity is a mystery for Freud, a fact for Lacan, and a cultural and political predicament for Mulvey and feminism.

Both Metz and Mulvey reached an understanding of visual culture that transcended the traditionally formalist readings of images and narrative. They both managed to combine a structuralist approach to the text as signifying system with a Freudian comprehension of the dynamics of intrasubjective structure. Both established that the enigma of sexual difference is central to the fantasies that circulate around vision and imagery, but it was Laura Mulvey who most fully explored the dynamics of power and fantasy that inform the gendering of the visual image. She concludes:

The structure of looking in narrative fiction film contains a contradiction in its own premises: the female image as a castration threat constantly endangers the unity of the diegesis and bursts through the world of illusion as an intrusive, static, one-dimensional fetish.[5]

The question of how the subordination of reality to a 'one-dimensional fetish' might be challenged remains central to a feminist practice. Obviously every genre of visual culture requires a different approach. Film-makers have experimented with different kinds of narrative and cinematography. Artists have explored different forms of textual self-consciousness and intertextuality. The photographers in 'What She Wants' have a common goal in representing gender otherwise. As such, this collection of artists is part of a new tradition which takes women's images of masculinity as a starting point. The images in this collection explore the varieties of fetishism with a light touch and humour, which is far from the 'one-dimensional', heavy, static, fixing characteristic of the fetishistic gaze. The good-natured curiosity and playfulness of the work counteracts the dreary sado-masochism of traditional fetishism.

PENIS ENVY: DOES IT EXIST?

The title of the exhibition and project 'What She Wants' is a reference to Freud's famous question 'What does woman want?'. The answer given by traditional psychoanalysis is that there is a certain state of mind which expresses an unconscious fantasy in which woman wants precisely what she imagines she lacks: a penis. This idea of penis envy has proved bothersome to feminists. Karen Horney suggests that penis envy is more a 'phallus envy', where women rightly envy or resent the cultural benefits of authority, mastery and power conferred on men in a patriarchal culture.

Lacanian feminists find that the ideology of contemporary culture replicates the state of mind of the pre-oedipal child – women are represented as 'not man', as lacking the phallus, and therefore as a threat to the narcissistic unity of infantile omnipotence. They argue that in cultural terms sexual difference is always represented in terms of a binary opposition in which masculinity is the norm and femininity is its 'other' or negation. The phallus becomes the signifier of difference, and the threat of its absence leads directly to the reinforcement of the boundaries of demarcated difference, through repetition, fetishism, polarization of difference, and especially the display of visible differences. Because sexual difference is understood as being, in part, a product of representation and the innate structure of language, the logic of this binary opposition is not amenable to change. 'Woman' must always bear the representation of lack and the (over)compensation for that lack.

If women identify within this system of phallic monism they necessarily pass through a stage of penis envy where their state of mind recapitulates that of the oedipal child for whom the phallus represents the desirable signifier of control. It may be that penis envy is as much a masculine predicament as a feminine one, when a man behaves like a boy for whom the father represents a desirable state of power, potency and authority.

A more emotionally dangerous state exists when a woman believes herself to be still a daughter, or when, wishing to regress to dependency, she idealizes a man to take on the role of a desired and envied father. Although this narrative is still the cultural 'norm' of traditional femininity and is thus an ideal for many women, if this predicament is acted out a woman can masochistically accept a role of powerlessness, depreciating her self and her own sexual identity.

Within the theory of phallic monism not only is 'penis envy' an inevitable structure of femininity but all other female desire stems from displacements of the impossible desire for the male organ, giving rise to a series of 'symbolic equations' in which penis = faeces = child = gift.

More recent, post-Freudian theories of subjectivity, which extend the excavation of subjectivity further back to the pre-oedipal archaeological layers of the mind that underlie the oedipal dynamics described by Freud, have shown that in masochism the punitive and sadistic father is very often a 'stand-in' for a desirable, all-giving mother. The absolute passivity and powerlessness that is the goal of many a masochistic fantasy is characteristic of the passivity of an infant in relation to the active mother. For a woman the idea of a dissolution of difference from the mother may be over-whelmingly threatening, and the penis is sought as protection from this.

Another approach is suggested by Maria Torok,[6] who points out that there is a ubiquitous human conviction that the sense of privation in the self is counterbalanced by the idea that others are enjoying themselves excessively. She wonders why it is that women, especially, are prone to being jealous and demanding, spiteful and despairing, inhibited and anxious (to list but some of the symptoms of this envy), when believing that men experience greater pleasure and enjoyment through their sexual identity, and then become contemptuous of themselves and other women. Dismissing the idea that there is any objective truth in this idealization of the penis she suggests that:

Though a seeming paradox at first, the fact is that in 'penis envy' nothing matters less than the penis itself. This part object appears to me as a stopgap invented to camouflage a desire, as an artificially constructed obstacle thrown in the way of our becoming one with ourselves in the course of being liberated from inhibited acts.[7]

For Torok there is a psychoanalytic tradition, which includes the work of Melanie Klein, Ernest Jones and Karen Horney, in which the subjectivity of early femininity is explored. This tradition does not stop at the theory of phallic monism but acknowledges that there is a parallel, gender-specific, developmental process in girls that includes the early discovery, and repression, of vaginal sensations. Linked to oedipal fantasies and guilt, the memories of early orgasmic sensations are repressed. Torok suggests that 'penis envy', or the discovery and idealization of boys' genitals, is often associated with the repressed memory of an orgasmic experience in girls. The penis envy is, therefore, a symptom. Torok concludes:

The symptom consists in idealising the penis, in investing it with all that one has lost hope of for oneself: one's own life project, that is genital maturity. This is what fulfilment means for the child, since she does not yet have it. Surely desire springs external, it never relents, yet it is forced to 'run on empty' or to fix itself in conventional images ... This is how envy emerges, envy of the idealised penis along with hatred for its supposed owner. Thus disappointment triumphs over love and frustration over fullness.[8]

'What She Wants' is a project in which sixty-four women artists look at men and communicate to one another about what they see. For the artists it is a 'liberation from inhibited acts', a liberation from the inhibition of impolite and curious looking and from the inhibition of transgressing the bounds of acceptable femininity. 'To want' is to give a direct active voice to the more indirect feminine activity of 'being wanted'. The 'she' that wants, implies the capacity for self-reflection through art which counteracts the stereotype of women as 'emotional and impulsive' creatures who live for love alone. That one can be both an 'I' and a 'she' is a fact of post-oedipal subjectivity, it can be either the tragedy of self-alienation or, as in the case of many of the works in this collection, the comedy of self-knowledge. Whilst objectifying man, the artists, nevertheless, do not lose sight of the corollary of the fact of divided subjectivity, the fact that the self can only reach full development through relationship with the other; the fact that full maturity implies an active encounter with the other. The collection of art here explores personal fantasies about sexual difference, and questions cultural stereotypes of masculinity and femininity. It raises a range of questions and explores a host of fantasies that are not included within canonical art practice. The work here is a metaphor for the complex issues of penis envy and representation; not only because some of the content is about the penis, but

because the processes and practices implied by this exhibition are themselves a celebration of 'inhibited acts'.

NOTES

1. Sigmund Freud, 'On Fetishism' (1927) in James Strachey (ed.), *The Complete Works of Sigmund Freud*, vol. 21, Hogarth, London 1953–73, pp. 152–3.
2. Ruth Mac Brunswick, 'The Preoedipal Phase of the Libido Development', *Psychoanalytic Quarterly*, IX, 1940, p. 304.
3. Laura Mulvey, 'You don't know what you're doing, do you Mr. Jones?', *Spare Rib* February 1973, pp. 13–16; also in Laura Mulvey, ed., *Visual and Other Pleasures*, Macmillan, London 1990.
4. Laura Mulvey, 'Visual Pleasures and Narrative Cinema', *Screen*, vol. 16, no. 3, autumn 1975; also in *Visual and Other Pleasures* and in Tony Bennett *et al.*, (eds), *Popular Film and Television*, Open University and British Film Institute 1981.
5. Mulvey, in *Popular Film and Television*, p. 214.
6. Maria Torok, 'The Meaning of "Penis Envy" in Women', in *Differences, A Journal of Feminist Cultural Studies*, vol. 4, spring 1992, special issue on 'The Phallus'.
7. Ibid., p. 5.
8. Ibid., p. 14.

MAPPING MALE BODIES:

THOUGHTS ON GENDERED AND

RACIALIZED LOOKING

Lola Young

A crucial aspect of the social interchange presided over by the networks of power which operate within this society concerns looking. As a generalization, men have looking privileges and rights which are not accorded to women, and these may be deployed to monitor, control and determine women's behaviour.

However, 'looking' is a highly complex set of processes and the privilege to which I refer vacillates according to the social categories and axes of power in which the people involved are located. Analysis of these issues, even if restricted to a male heterosexual look at women, has to take account of how it may be differentiated according to the social status of the men who look and the women at whom they look. The aim of this chapter is to raise some questions regarding how looking may be racialized, using both historical and contemporary examples, and to indicate how the mystique surrounding the penis is being challenged by the practices of women image-makers.

From the late eighteenth century, white bourgeois men who belonged to the emerging class of professional scientists could subject black women to exacting anatomical examinations: at the same time black women's bodies were publicly displayed in Europe. One of the documented instances of such a degrading exhibition was that of Sarah Bartmann. Born in southern Africa and displayed all over Europe, she was called the Hottentot Venus; her very name indicating the comparison of what was held to be an African aesthetic deficiency with classical European standards of female beauty. The bulk of such investigatory work was effected by male scientists, but the results of this 'research' were available to anyone who could afford to pay the price of a ticket to view women like Bartmann.[1] The European male desire to demystify and control the female body had limited acceptability with regard to white women: with the institutionalization of black people's inferior status, few such inhibitions existed.

When white women wished to exercise their privileged racial status through the right to look at black male bodies, the issue was, unsurprisingly, more contentious. White women who looked at black men were characterized as having a prurient sexual curiosity and were seen as 'racial traitors', as is revealed by the following comment from a popular magazine article published in 1917:

Some years ago we used to have large bodies of natives sent from Africa on military service or in some travelling show, and it was a revelation of horror and disgust to behold the manner in which English women would flock to see these men ... a scandal and a disgrace to English womanhood. How then is it possible to maintain as the one stern creed in the policy of the Empire the eternal supremacy of white over black?[2]

Here the links between black male sexuality and accepted norms of feminine propriety, and the putative effects on the imperial project, are made clear. Delicate English womanhood was not to be subjected to the debilitating effects of gazing upon the black male phallus. The power associated with the right to looking upon the Other as a sexual object was a privilege which was strictly for white bourgeois men. There are indications that it is not acceptable for black women to look on black men's secrets either. Although not specifically referring to the body, there is a curious incident in an old Paul Robeson film, *Song of Freedom*, where his screen wife, Ruth (Elizabeth Welch) breaks the taboo regarding gazing upon the 'witch doctor's' inner sanctum: for having betrayed patriarchal traditions she must be punished. Although Ruth attempts to conform to the norms of 'primitive' village life in Africa, she contravenes a major taboo by looking on that which is forbidden. Mandingo – the witch doctor – and his secret rituals are not available to the Europeanized black female gaze (or indeed, to any other female's gaze). It is significant that it should be the forbidden look which is implicated here, in view of the implications regarding power: to seize the right to look is to attempt to seize power. The biblical referent for this incident might be the curse of Ham, whose gaze upon his naked father in a drunken stupor caused God to curse his successors with blackness thereafter. It was posited that this curse 'explained' blackness as an attribute of Africans.[3]

There is still an underlying notion that nudity – particularly for men – signifies black and/or primitive savagery as opposed to white civilization, and it has always been more acceptable for black women and men to appear naked for public viewing in societies where bodies are meant to be kept hidden. The 'savages' and 'primitives' displayed, whether in medical and scientific texts, exhibitions of 'native' life, eugenicist and anthropological photography or, as is still the case today, in anthropological television films, are frequently considered as the atavistic remnants of a primeval past. Clothes signify progress, culture and potency.

The quotation regarding white women and African male bodies is a historical example, but the anxiety engendered by women seizing the (phallic) camera and using it to explore any man's body is still obvious in contemporary Western societies. As Richard Dyer has pointed out, the reversal of the look – that is, women looking sexually at men – violates the rules established by men's power base.[4] Such a violation is intensified by looking upon the nude male: being naked connotes powerlessness and a return to infantile vulnerability; not feelings commensurate with dominance and authority.

According to Dyer, 'the greatest instability of all for the male image ... is the fact that the penis isn't a patch on the phallus. The penis can never live up to the mystique implied by the phallus.'[5] It is this mystique which the interdiction on public display of the erect penis is supposed to preserve, but what does an erection amount to that it needs to be so protected? A briefly achieved, difficult to maintain and control physical reaction, which is not even the greatest source of sexual pleasure for many women. The prohibition on viewing it is necessary *because* the reality simply cannot live up to the mythology.

Although there are now magazines ostensibly aimed at women for whom the display of the nude male body is their reason for existence, it is hard to claim that these actively subvert conventional notions of the association of power and masculinity. North American *Playgirl*'s current idea of the ideal male is that of a musclebound huge-thighed man, usually under thirty, full of arrogant self-confidence, perhaps astride a Harley Davidson or in the gymnasium: there is still the presence of a phallic symbol and still the attempt to sustain the belief that men are never passive, they are always just about to spring into action ... not much change there. Sarah Kent observes:

The answer lies, I think, in power relations between the sexes and between viewer and viewed. Once a female observer is envisaged, her presence becomes a conscious element in the encoding of the image. The tensions, ambiguities and contradictions apparent in the male-pin-up reflect a conflict of interests that is fundamental to this new interaction. The male model apparently puts himself at the disposal of the female viewer, while actually trying to maintain a position of sexual dominance.[6]

Ironically, although these nude males are often positioned in such a way as to deny their passivity, the ultimate physical confirmation of their active sexuality is precisely that which is prohibited: erections are still taboo even in the liberated pages of *Playgirl*.

Most of the heterosexual women I know who are interested in sexually stimulating material find little to excite in magazines such as *For Women* and *Playgirl*. The juxtaposition of articles exhorting female readers to seize control of their lives, to be decisive, and the phallocentric photographic compositions is an uneasy one. The concentration on men with over-developed musculature suggests rampant male narcissism rather than an attempt to engage with women's sexual fantasies and aspirations. Anecdotal evidence suggests that there is not much in these magazines to undermine or circumvent male supremacy, except in the way in which some of the images are used as objects of derision by the alleged targeted audience. The homo-erotic appeal of the images is not something which would be highlighted by those who market such magazines, since to discuss the pleasures that men might enjoy through looking at other male bodies is another proscribed subject.

As a generalization then, the right to look at women's bodies is an entitlement that has been primarily enjoyed by bourgeois white men as part of their patriarchal power. Historically, whether under the guise of scientific investigation or the production of visual culture, it is white bourgeois men who have had privileged access to looking rights.

For black men living under the institution of slavery and later under segregationist rule in North America, the right to look at white women was an emotionally charged and sexually fraught act, liable to bring them to the attention of a lynching mob. Under North American and British slavery, black men could look at black women under conditions determined and controlled by white slave-owners. The traces of this colonial history in regard to attitudes towards black men looking at white women are evident in contemporary culture where prohibitions around interracial sexual relations still abound.

The European myth of the excessive dimensions of black male genitalia has contributed to a seemingly endless number of anxious anecdotes and jokes, and constructed a situation where it is impossible to draw, paint, film or photograph black men in the nude, with their penises exposed, without such an image being overburdened with meaning. Thus, for example, although readings of Mapplethorpe's photographs of black men's penises may vary from critic to critic, or from context to context, it is always acknowledged and understood that his images of black men's genitalia carry with them a set of meanings which are inextricably bound to white European racial and sexual anxieties.[7]

For both black and white women, an excursion into this territory is fraught with complex problems of myth, history, intention, interpretation, racism, sexism and so on. So perhaps it is not surprising to note that the complete black male nude is apparently too dangerous to depict for an artist who is acutely aware of the political implications of her image making. Are similar issues articulated in the commercial world of magazine photographic production and if so, how?

A recent British example of some of the complexities raised by the analysis of gender, sex and 'race' in contemporary visual culture is a feature in *Marie Claire* based on interviews with, and photographs of, thirteen men: the subject is men and their feelings about their bodies.[8] Since, in many discussions about male genitalia, bigger is almost invariably associated with better, several of the men were reported as being concerned with their lack of height and the size of their penises. All but one of the men have their faces obscured and are shown full length, from the front and behind. The only man whose face we see is James, a young black man, a student who likes his body best 'from my neck to my knees'.[9] James merits a whole page, assuming a delicate dance pose, one hand on his hip, one on his lower thigh, as if to mark out the parameters of his body that he *really* likes. James's photograph is the only full-length one of a male that does not show his penis, and the artistic pretensions of the composition and lighting is of a different quality from the more utilitarian, almost medicalized shots of the other men. Although there is another black man, David, featured in the smaller shots, the lighting and quality of the photographs serve to homogenize the colour of the nude bodies presented. David is captioned with the quotation 'I've got a lovely arse – something you can grab on to', a theme elaborated on in the two paragraphs which follow another, smaller version of his naked body. David informs us that he's got a 'nice penis. A reasonable size. I won't say big, that would be boasting.'[10] Of course we do not know the circumstances of these interviews or the context in which these words were spoken: what is interesting is what has been selected as print-worthy for each subject and it is notable that the association of sexual satisfaction and genitalia are most emphasized in David's account of his attitude to his body. Other men complain that their penises are too small or do not mention them specifically and only Colin articulates the view that 'it's not the size that matters, it's the performance'.[11] David's assertion that to say his penis is big would be boasting, invokes the historical racialization of male genitalia.

In the March 1992 USA issue of *Playgirl* there is a spread featuring a black model, Greg Ducre or 'Atlas reborn' according to his *Playgirl* soubriquet. This classical reference is intended to lend credibility to the artistic pretensions of the photography and to play down the rather tacky associations of soft pornography: the Graeco-Roman tradition of displaying the strong, athletic, male nude, and in this instance, as like a god, is often called upon to sell commodities. A feature of Greg's photoset is that it appears to have been shot with a dark grey filter which elides the difference between his skin colour and the backcloth. It is as if he is about to be absorbed into the background which is where his racial status places him in North American society – unless, that is, he excels in particular professions: notably, sport or popular entertainment. The reader is invited to guess Greg's occupation from the following clue: 'What does dramatic, dark and *dangerously* sexy Greg have in common with Fred Astaire, Mikhail Baryshnikov and Rudolph Nureyev?' (my italics). *Playgirl* assumes we are sufficiently knowledgeable about European culture to recognize that the white men cited are all dancers, and, of course, this is one of the spheres where black people are expected to excel. We are to conclude then, that this 'boy', Greg's, vocation is dancing, a term replete with sexual connotations, especially when associated with black men.[12]

The images in *Playgirl* and *Marie Claire* have been discussed in order to indicate how discourses on the male body are racialized in contemporary visual culture, and to suggest how the historical circumstances of colonialism and racism still permeate contemporary discursive practices. The conjunction of 'race' and sex makes it difficult to render an image of the black man's genitalia that is not saturated with the myth of black men's hypersexuality. (This is not, by the way, to imply that it is ever possible to produce an image of a 'real', essential black, subject which is outside of ideology.) To be more specific, the meanings which have accrued to black male genitalia have produced a situation where women photographers with an awareness of the historical and contemporary material effects of racist ideologies – whether black or white – wishing to make work using black men are placed in a difficult position, and black men's bodies are effectively relegated to the status of forbidden territory. Perhaps this is uncomfortably close to the Freudian notion of white women's sexuality as the 'dark continent', but it does strike me as curious that so few black men are featured in the 'What She Wants' exhibition.

A woman who constructs images of male bodies in her photography is likely to encounter anxious responses from men. The attempt at humour in the headline 'Men get raw deal in new art show' exemplifies the defensiveness brought about in men by nude male bodies on display.[13] As well as being about an uneasiness which surrounds the homo-erotic potential of such images, much of this anxiety is due to the fact that so many women do think of penises as a comical feature of human anatomy. What is it about men's naked bodies that seems to be so funny to so many women?

If it is the case that we laugh at that which we are attempting to repress, because it stimulates unacceptable reactions, or that which is strange, what does this humorous banter mean in relation to women viewing penises? According to Freud, jokes may be divided into the non-tendentious and the tendentious joke: the notion of the tendentious joke is most relevant here. As the term implies, the tendentious joke is constructed with a purpose in mind, and the purpose behind the joke is generally one which, were it to be expressed freely, would incur disapproval. The disapproval may be externally generated – by friends, family or society in general – or it may be that there is an internal constraint being placed on the thought expressed through the joke. In the tendentious joke the pleasure is derived from joke-making and communicating with others, material which is subject to social condemnation and would otherwise be repressed.

Much of the work in this exhibition implicitly acknowledges that penises and erections are not as crucial for an expression of sexuality as we have been led to believe, but it is not only in 'What She Wants' that this humour is apparent. Joanna Quinn's animation, *Girl's Night Out* (1992) captures the ribald hilarity of women's responses to looking at men's naked bodies, as does the exuberant commentary by North American and British women on the soundtrack of Jo Menell's short film *Dick* (1989). This humorous approach highlights the inherent contradiction referred to earlier: that despite representing potency, and strength, the penis is the most tender part of male anatomy, constantly having to be protected both from physical attack and public scrutiny. For women who have learned the extent of men's psychological investment in this anatomical representation of their sexual identity, humour and irony are subversive strategies in the struggle against phallic dominance.

What about the pleasures of image-making and looking? Scopophilia – that is, the sexually motivated pleasure taken in looking – is not the sole preserve of men: women photographers can and have affirmed their sexual pleasure in taking sexualized images of men's bodies. Neither is sadomasochistic violence and there are many ways in which images may be constructed and enjoyed by women viewers that are both subtle and explicit suggestions of the powerful sexual fantasies which many women experience.

Liz Kotz points to a strategy for defamiliarizing images which is not dependent on notions of 'truthful' or 'realistic' images:

Rather than contesting representation in terms of content ... strategies of repetition and proliferation offer means of subverting the referential logic that underpins representation, of emptying the referent of its meaning, of its status *as* representation.[14]

Such a strategy recognizes the difficulties in trying to evacuate the old meanings and construct fresh ones from representations of male bodies when it is inescapably the site of struggle for long and complex histories of gender, class, 'race' and sexual orientation. Chris Duyt, one of the exhibitors who did photograph a black man, commented: 'If I reverse the focus of much pornography from "cunt" to "cock" – I may repeat the stereotype of the "big black dick"', and seems to suggest that there may be possible a level of identification between her as a white woman and the black man due to the sexual objectification of their bodies. If there is a possibility of such an identification, then it has to be predicated on a recognition of how such issues may be intensified for black women photographers who are doubly determined as hypersexual through their gender and through their racial designation.

As well as those forms of socially constructed identifications mentioned above, there are the aesthetic notions of what constitutes beautiful bodies to engage with too. Women image-makers are attempting to map male bodies without recourse to the conventional phallocentric codes of male nude photography, and defying normative approaches to representing the male body. Women are making progress in exploring the structures and processes of power embedded in imaging the male body (as well as their own) and claiming the right to do so on their own terms, and because that is about taking control, it is an urgent, political task.

NOTES

1. Even after her death in 1815, Sarah Bartmann's genitalia were put on display in the Musée de l'Homme in Paris and were still available to the public gaze until at least 1985. See Sander L. Gilman, *Difference and Pathology: Stereotypes of Sexuality, Race and Madness*, Cornell University, New York 1985, pp. 85–8.

2. From *Titbits* magazine, 21 July 1917, quoted in Fernando Henriques, *Children of Caliban: Miscegenation*, Secker and Warburg, London 1974, p. 141.

3. See Peter Fryer, *Staying Power: The History of Black People in Britain*, Pluto Press, London 1984; and Sander L. Gilman, *Sexuality: An Illustrated History*, John Wiley and Sons, New York 1989.

4. This does not necessarily mean that 'looking' is always active and powerful, and that 'being looked at' is always passive and powerless. Women and men may derive pleasure from being looked at and be able to exploit the position accorded to a desired object. See Richard Dyer, 'Don't Look Now', *Screen*, vol. 23, 3–4, September/October 1982, p. 63.

5. Ibid., p. 72.

6. Sarah Kent, 'The Erotic Male Nude' in S. Kent and J. Morreau (eds), *Women's Images of Men*, Writers' and Readers', London 1985, pp. 75–105.

7. I am thinking here of the way in which Mapplethorpe's photographs are used as a backdrop, rather than a dominant motif in Isaac Julien's film *Looking for Langston* (1987). See Kobena Mercer and Isaac Julien, 'True Confessions: A Discourse on Images of Black Male Sexuality' in *Critical Decade: Black British Photography in the 80s*,

Ten.8 Photo Paperback, Vol. 2 No. 3, spring 1992, pp. 40–9; see also Kent, pp. 85–6.

8. *Marie Claire*, July 1991, pp. 22–8.

9. Ibid., p. 22.

10. Ibid., p. 28.

11. Ibid., p. 28.

12. *Playgirl: Entertainment for Women*, March 1992, pp. 68–73.

13. *Yorkshire Post*, 2 August 1993.

14. Liz Kotz 'Complicity: Women Artists Investigating Masculinity' in Pamela Church Gibson and Roma Gibson (eds), *Dirty Looks*, British Film Institute, London 1993, p. 106.

WHAT SHE WANTS

AND WHAT SHE GETS

Cherry Smyth

'What She Wants' establishes a site for women to take their pleasure seriously, eschewing market demands for images replete with fake seductiveness, which fail to 'clitillate'. The show attempts to chart current changing masculinities and situates 'want' back into the discourse of straight feminism, beyond the tortured defensiveness of anti-porn feminism and the laissez faire transgression of some pro-sex representations.

Even a couple of years ago such a project would have been constrained by women's fears of colluding with an oppressive system of looking, of indulging in a luxury that feminism could ill afford, or of trying to imitate the clichéd codes of porn in a didactic demonstration of revenge.

WHAT WE GET

In response to Freud's infamous question, 'What does woman want?', this exhibition begins to assert what some women want in a vibrant and diverse visual language that contests the dominant meanings of masculinity and pushes the formal confines of the photographic medium. From Mars

Gomes's large photo-paint canvasses (p. 147) and Cathy Ward's exquisite 3D acrylic and cloth pieces (p. 105), to Naomi Salaman's X-ray dicks (p. 130) and Justine Garratty's goofy pop collages (p. 107), the work boasts rich experimentation as well as more conventional black-and-white figurative work. Ann Rogers's use of body paint to define and parody 'muscles' is witty and satisfying (p. 146).

Themes run from enticing voyeurism by Sharita Rao (p. 102), to cosy intimates by Iona Fabian, who introduces Ivan (p. 80), and Harriet Thompson, who reveals 'ex Lover Paul' (pp. 114, 115). Transvestism recurs in work by Fiona Lord and Grace Lau (pp. 104, 108), and Sue Evans's sexy and astounding 'Venus De Milo' (p. 75), while Linda Chapman poses her subject with his cock between his legs (or removed) suggesting an hermaphrodite or a transsexual (p. 144).

Gender-associated metaphors, such as 'Mother Nature' and female forms and genitalia as food, are interrogated in many of the pieces, such as Nadege Meriau's androgynous man in nature (p. 94) and the edible penis as fruit by Tabitha Goode (p. 112). Herlinde Koelbl's blunt and uncompromising images, 'Cockerel Cock', powerfully extend the metaphor of 'cockerel' to its literal expression (pp. 126, 127). She uses a lush and handsome cockerel placed between a man's legs to suggest erection. Its plush feathers and dark comb evoke pubic hair and balls, with the slight twist of a suggestion of red, fleshy labia in the wrinkled skin. The proud gaze and 'cocked' head of the bird lend a majestic resilience and questioning quality to the hidden penis. The alertness of the huge live bird with its open beak evokes an extremely strong presence of an erect cock. But its power to threaten is temporary, which seems to represent one of the major crises of masculinity – the unsustainability of erection. In the next shot the bird is dead, its neck in a mute curve against the man's leg, its feathers shaped around the limp (now visible) cock like a cape, a head-dress. The moment is almost post-coital. Has the man shot the bird, wrung its neck, or fucked it? The word 'crestfallen' will never appear the same again.

Some of the more conceptual work is very humorous. Diane Baylis's 'Who's Afraid of the Big Bad Wolf?', Kay Hart's 'Sammy', and Hermione Wiltshire's 'Still, Flying', with its magical, flying dildo, keenly mock how we read phallic images (pp. 124, 131, 136), while Flo Fox's techno-cock emerging from the computer monitor like a fusby, soft creature is gloriously funny (p. 79).

Just what is 'Adam's Secret' (Sally Griffyn, p. 143)? That he shaves his pubes, has several piercings on his cock, enjoys a huge ring stretching down his balls, or that he has a tiny bell on one of the rings? Does it tinkle when he walks? The dainty bell sits beautifully beside the implacable balls-ring, while the exposure of his shaved skin is undeniably tender against the metal. Here we witness a fastidious commitment to the body and a statement of defiance in the face of cases like the recent Operation Spanner in which gay men were imprisoned for consensual SM sex.

Isn't it surprising that only one artist directly addresses safer sex and that there are no images of an eroticized condom? Does this relative absence point up the generalized worry about penetrative sex in a time of AIDS? Or does it suggest that too many heterosexual women in this country still see themselves as relatively low-risk? Or do we have to have images of safer sex, to have safer sex? Perhaps it is because, in spite of vigorous attempts by AIDS organizations to eroticize condoms, many women still find them unpleasant to smell and touch and consider them a/side of, not a part of, the erotic exchange?

That so much of the work is set in interiors – domestic and studio – reinforces the private sexual space of female hetero/sexuality. The intense texturality of Robin Shaw's close-ups of penis skin, for example, constructs a microscopic landscape of intricate beauty and fragility (pp. 128, 129).

HUMILIATE ME PLEASE

In 1980 a season of women artists' work called 'Women's Images of Men' showed at the ICA, then toured the country. The artists, asked to respond to the question 'How Do You See Men?' sent in pieces which revealed great tenderness and compassion towards men, as well as exposing their emotional dependency, violence and absurd posturing. The show however caused enormous controversy and some abuse, as many critics perceived it as a collective expression of the desire to humiliate and destroy men, to take revenge on them as objects. Although there were only twenty male nudes out of a total of ninety-eight works, critics lamented the 'veritable forest of penises'[1] and misunderstood the representation of the penis as a symbol of male power.

As 'What She Wants' focuses on men as objects of erotic pleasure, very few of the works exhibit the hostility associated with 'man-hating feminism', though undoubtedly some will be read as such by the more insecure. For some artists the role reversal is undeniably charged.

Through the medium of the lens, I enjoyed the role-reversal power of manipulating my male nudes, of dominating an erotic scenario, of being director and producer.[2]

Two pieces by Yanna Papaioannou explore notions of dominance and irreverence (pp. 110, 111). In one, 'The Audition', a bare-assed man sits on a wooden floor. Someone (a woman we presume), stretches his penis out between her thumb and forefinger. Although the image itself is cruel, the lighting is soft honey orange, setting up a delicious visual irony between the harshness of her action and the warm seductiveness of the mood. It plays on notions of penis size, echoing the kind of remarks men make about breast size. There is no sense that the man has not consented to be measured for the part. In 'Overstep', the man lies legs apart as a woman's foot squashes his penis and balls into a soft pile of skin and flesh. It is disturbing, but invites a desire to protect those vulnerable, exposed parts. Again the image is constructed to act as a calculated metaphor for anger, dismissal, humiliation, but the rich-coloured lighting undercuts its apparent violence.

In Karen F's 'Untitled' piece (p. 139), which shows eight small black-and-white images of a man with his hands and feet bound, once more violence is controlled, subdued. The subject is immobilized, made safe, made still and emits no sense of having been forcibly restrained. These are not didactic statements, but rather knowing explorations of submission which could encourage the fe/male spectator to rethink passivity and vulnerability.

In Katharine Meynell's 'Vampire Seat' (p. 120), we meet humour head-on. Here we have an ordinary wooden dining chair. In the centre of its black seat, slightly to the front, is positioned a small glass rectangular screen. There is a sound of lapping and the image of a man's mouth, his fat, thin, wide, narrow tongue licking, slobbering, tonguing the screen. Have a seat, do. From ass-licking to a delightful evocation of an oral sex machine, this video installation is one of the most concise, effective works of its kind. This mouth is captured and programmed for your pleasure.

TAKE THE TOYS FROM THE BOYS

While there has been a shift away from the monolithic essentialism of bad men, good feminists, there has also been relative silence from straight feminists and straight men on how men are changing. Not only do women get the chance to own an active gaze, but the male models want to be gazed at.

Young men are being sold images which rupture traditional icons of masculinity. They are stimulated to look at themselves — and other men — as objects of consumer desire. They are getting pleasures previously branded taboo or feminine.[3]

This exchange of looks between men continues to be highly problematized by homophobia, which still prevents some straight men from allowing themselves to be 'caught looking' at images of other men. As Eamonn McCabe (Picture Editor of the *Guardian*) commented on a recent *Woman's Hour* programme:

Am I allowed to look? With the whole gay culture, what would someone like myself [*sic*] be doing looking at a whole room of male nudes? I would find it really difficult to study and enjoy them.[4]

While there are developed discourses around lesbian and gay and black sexualities, there is still limited self-knowledge in discourses around white, heterosexual masculinity: 'Masculinity remains somewhat removed, like a crumbling castle around which the battle against the Other rages – the cause but not the site of the struggle.'[5]

From photographers like Robert Mapplethorpe, Herb Ritts, Sunil Gupta and Rotimi Fani-Kayode to film-makers like Derek Jarman and Isaac Julien, there is a rich vein of images to mine. Women, however, have little or no tradition of erotic images of men taken by other women. As Nayland Blake comments, straight artists from Marky Mark to Madonna are 'positioning themselves with all the signification of gay male sexuality in order to make themselves read as sexual'. He goes on: 'explicit heterosexual imagery is now so commonplace that it no longer carries the weight of sexuality'.[6]

Although there is little space here fully to explore what constitutes a homoerotic image, just consider the recent Britvic Orange billboard advertisement, which showed an extremely well-endowed fairy, camply waving a wand over a pack of juice. The marketing office was surprised to learn of its homo-erotic appeal when challenged by the *Pink Paper* (July 1993), arguing that they had wanted a gentle image to appeal to women. That they used gay artists Pierre and Gilles didn't seem to be an issue. Images inspired by a gay male aesthetic sell products.

The increased vulnerability of the gay male body since the AIDS epidemic began has invested many artists with increased sensitivity and a sense of the body as unbearably mortal. Curator Naomi Salaman acknowledges the ambiguous influence exerted by gay male images: 'I started off my research for "What She Wants" cautiously envious of gay male culture and the eruption of sex celebration that seems to be taking place.'[7]

Photographer Robin Shaw, however, works against the dominant codes of gay male representations of the male nude:

Soft porn available for women now is based on a gay model for the men's market and for me, it does not turn me on whatsoever because it doesn't hook into my experience of male sexuality. The only pictures available of men were these hairless hunks.[8]

The preponderance of the homosexual male object certainly informs the work of some of the artists who inscribe their work with the sexual cues and codes of homo-eroticism. Brigitte Mayer's 'David' evokes Caravaggio with its lush tones and serene gaze, while her 'Last Supper' is a delightfully camp appropriation of the disciples as naked gay servants (pp. 73, 125). The pale face make-up, dark, sullen lips and direct gaze are quietly confrontational, without being intimidatory. This is, surprisingly, one of the few group shots in the show. When you consider the popular phenomenon of 'fag-hags' and the alleged arousal straight women get from looking at images of men making love, we might have anticipated a wider exploration of this theme.

Moira McIver's 'Seductive Myths' (p. 133) can also be read as homo-erotic, with her use of uniforms and pale exposed flesh, which conjure the acute tension of danger, pride and mortality. That the bodies are in repose, yet still uniformed, suggests that at any moment they may have to be instantly alert, defensive, 'erect'. They may have to kill to survive. Their hyper-masculinity is offset by the tender, freckled skin. The eroticization of the ass also resonates with homosex as in Honey Salvadori's 'Archaos' (p. 77) – a raunchy, energetic image of the ass, thinly veiled under a muslin skirt, gripped by a hand from off-frame. Only the peach fuzz on the man's ass defines his gender, while the image is open to a multiplicity of readings across gender and sexualities.

The upfront female fisting/fist-fucking image by Jacqueline Kennedy, euphemistically called 'Other Chambers' (p. 138), manages to instil peace and gentleness into an act usually associated with exertion or force. The woman's hand on the man's hip is resting, not grasping, making the action seem 'everyday'.

The pieces most overtly influenced by a queer aesthetic are undoubtedly Cathy Ward's tactile, perverse embellishments of the male torso. Crowned in a swathe of daisies in 'Sunshine', body-painted in short, straight strokes in 'Enmesh', haloed by a rash of white dashes of fat paint in 'Pure' and latticed by cut-out paper against a deep purple in 'Play Jack Pudding', the male bodies burst with vitality and colour (pp. 105, 106). Ward raids photographic images from gay male porn magazines, exaggerates their

Greek classical poses and muscle-flexing, and lays them in highly decorative canvases and frames. Ward explains:

I attempted to lattice-cut these brutally naked renditions of the male physique into delicately Wicker-like, utilitarian forms. The flimsy filigree of the paper contrasts with the strong, assertive stance posed in the photographs. The body patterning comments on the current interest in tribal scarification, piercing and tattooing, as well as the gym-crazed worshipping of physical perfection, which has developed in some cases into a ritualistic punishing of the flesh.

These luscious, extravagant works make the male body iconic, delivering it up as an exotic food, a sacrificial offering to anyone tantalized enough to taste.

DON'T LOOK NOW

For many white gay men, the ability to be looked at is well developed and has been less fraught with the power imbalances of the heterosexual gaze. For black gay men, looking at each other, or being the object of the white gaze, it's another story.

Heterosexual masculinity shifts its problems and anxieties, defining them as belonging to others. Our identity represents its own problems in the image of the compliant female, the black man as sexual savage and the perverted homosexual.[9]

As Isaac Julien and Kobena Mercer assert in 'Male Order', the white homo-erotic gaze is also riven with stereotypes of the hypersexual black stud and the mute, passive, exotic Asian. The scarcity of black artists and black images in the show, plus the total absence of images of Asian men, denote the persistent fear of mis/representing the black subject. The black/ Asian man is so over-determined by racist myths about black sexuality that the weight of this colonial legacy is hard to shift. As Kobena Mercer argues in his thorough re-examination of Mapplethorpe's work:

Mapplethorpe's scopic fixation on the luxurious beauty of black skin thus implies a kind of 'negrophilia', an aesthetic idealisation of racial difference that merely inverts and reverses the binary axis of colonial discourse, in which all things black are equated with darkness, dirt and danger, as manifest in the psychic representations of 'negrophobia'. Both positions, whether they overvalue or devalue the visible signs of racial difference, inhabit the shared space of colonial fantasy.[10]

One of the more striking images of black men is Sue Fox's portrait of the head and naked torso of 'Buyaka' (p. 97). The black subject smiles directly into the camera, his face confident, eyes shining. It is a relaxed, easy pose, a simple portrait. Does it matter if the photographer is white or black? Do we want to know, find ourselves guessing? As long as we ask these questions, which we don't pose of the white subject, it signals that the black subject is still held in deep anxiety. We want to trust that the photographic process has not abused or compromised him. Is this protectiveness empathy, or part of a discourse of patronizing emasculation by me as a white woman? While there are some images of black men, there are significantly no black penises.

In the phantasmic space of the white male imaginary, the big black phallus is perceived as a threat not only to hegemonic white masculinity, but to Western civilisation itself, since the 'bad object' represents a danger to white womanhood and therefore the threat of miscegenation, eugenic pollution and racial degeneration.[11]

There is a cautious attempt to articulate this absence by Chris Duyt in 'Untitled' (p. 145). We see four prints of extreme close-ups of black skin framed in a rectangle. There are tight curls of hair and wrinkles which could be neck wrinkles or wrinkles at the base of the penis. Both readings are erotic, as both areas have erotogenic potential. In the centre of the rectangle where the four images meet is a blur. The head/penis is missing. Is it impossible for black or white women to frame the black penis directly? Or has the context of a predominantly white show made black artists reluctant to exhibit their work for fear of colluding with a white gaze?

VICARIOUS PLEASURES

Riddled with complex contradictions, the reversal of power relations is a necessary step towards a greater sexual equality that involves humility and respect from both sides. Too much of 'what we want' is unspoken, regulated, censored in the name of 'family values' and 'protecting other women and children'. Women artists are employing less didacticism and more irony to subvert dominant male attitudes, and there are signs of a strengthening female aesthetic that is unapologetic, imaginative, daring and fresh.

'What She Wants' convinces with authority and conviction that to depict female desire for men does not simply involve reversing the codes men use on our bodies, but requires the invention of new ones, formally and metaphorically. It forces us to rethink passivity and power and recognize that men are willing to collude in the pleasure women take in them as beauties, hunks, lovers, boys, queers, friends, trannies, weaklings and sex machines. It also demonstrates the multiple identities of fascinating masculinities which invite fetishization across sexualities and gender. In 'What She Wants', women have the power and space to eschew the fears of objectification and locate and relish their visual and sexual eroticism in bits, w/holes, and cocks, for all of us to celebrate.

NOTES

1. Sarah Kent and J. Morreau (eds), *Women's Images of Men*, Writers and Readers, London 1985, p. 20.
2. G. Lau, 'Perversion Through the Camera', *New Formations*, No. 19, spring 1993, p. 45.
3. F. Mort, 'Boy's Own? Masculinity, Style and Popular Culture', in R. Chapman and J. Rutherford (eds), *Male Order*, Lawrence and Wishart, London 1988, p. 194.
4. E. McCabe, *Woman's Hour*, Radio Four, 10 August 1993.
5. J. Rutherford and R. Chapman 'The Forward March of Men Halted', *Male Order*, p. 11.
6. N. Blake, 'Believe me, Everybody has Something Pierced in California: an interview with Nayland Blake' by Stephen Johnstone and John Gange in *New Formations*, no. 19, spring 1993, p. 67.

7. N. Salaman; 'Women's Art Practice, Man's Sex', *Variant* 12, 1992.

8. R. Shaw, *Woman's Hour*, Radio Four, 10 August 1993.

9. J. Rutherford, *Male Order*, p. 23.

10. K. Mercer, 'Just Looking For Trouble', in Lynne Segal and Mary McIntosh (eds), *Sex Exposed: Sexuality and the Pornography Debate*, Virago, London 1992, p. 99.

11. Ibid., p. 100.

Part Two

INTRODUCTION

Naomi Salaman

'What She Wants' was developed in response to the anti-pornography arguments of the late 1980s, to explore the other side of the debate in terms of visual practice. The initial aim was to complicate the fixed categories, expectations and criticisms of pornography in which woman is assumed to be the (passive) object of the gaze and man the (active) viewer.

The exhibition is conceived as an experimental reversal of erotic traditions, consisting of photographic work by over sixty women artists selected from an open submission held over the summer of 1992.

Photography has taken over as the prevailing popular medium of representing the desired body, and it inherits a gendered tradition from the figurative arts. The gender divide is increased by the ways in which women have had limited access to the technology of photography. Although snapshot photography is available to all, studio and commercial practice is still overwhelmingly male-dominated.

The motivation for collating a survey show of this kind is to redress a number of imbalances and dispel a number of myths about the male body and the female observer. Questions raised relate to the practice of making explicit images; what is public, what is private, what is art, what is obscenity, why is the sexualized male body still so taboo? Presented here is a range of ways of looking at men and masculinity, exploring new ways of articulating and empowering an aesthetics of sexed subjectivity.

No one will be able to attend the exhibition or flip through this selection of images and find out what women want. There is no single way to read an image, just as there is no basis for assuming that what one woman likes will please another. The idea of the show is to open out the cultural implications of 'what she wants' as dynamic connections in representation and sexuality, which cannot be reduced to an image. Rather than being a show by and for heterosexual women, 'What She Wants' works away at the sense of heterosexuality, in a way to un-think the assumed stability of gender identity.

Recently there has been an upsurge in media, advertising and entertainment made for women which uses images of near-naked men. This, combined with the new women's pornography magazines, has given women the opportunity to look publicly at men for their pleasure. This new access to images of men has opened up many questions about looking, which the artists in the show have responded to.

The permission to look operates on a number of different levels, between fantasies of bad behaviour and forms of real censorship. One woman rang the exhibition office to say she was worried about photographing her boyfriend's erection because she thought it was illegal. Of course an erection is not illegal and neither is her photographing it. What she does with those photographs may, on the other hand, get her in trouble with the law. Another artist spoke of having her negatives returned from the photo lab, which refused to print what it considered to be 'pornography'. Here we have a familiar scenario where someone who has a small amount of power makes a judgement based on what is and what is not acceptable to them personally, and then acts on it as if it were the law. Women need to feel confident and serious about their art practice in order to resist the constraints of petty officialdom which will persistently evoke non-existent laws about photographs of naked men or erections.

Another area of permission is at a more ethical level. Can a good feminist exploit a male model in the manner which seems similar to the much-criticized commodification and objectification of women? Will the woman allow herself to look? Will she be true to her curiosity about the male body and her visual pleasure, or will she submit to her fear of transgressing an ideal model of behaviour? If she cannot let herself look, she will refuse to objectify but does she not end up confirming the gender stereotype, that men look and women are looked at?

This dilemma is further played out after the first two levels of permission have been worked through, by the exchange of looks and directorial power that operate during a photographic shoot. In order to arrive at the desired image the woman artist has to direct camera, lights and model to her vision. This involves more than just allowing herself to look: here we have the need for her to impose her ideas, to adjust everything until it is right for her. Of course this is a familiar scenario for any photographer. However, it is unusual that the photographer is female and the model male. The context, too, is unconventional: neither a commercial shoot nor an established art practice. Brought into play here is the gender transgression of the woman telling the man what to do for her visual satisfaction. This interaction brings some of the theoretical concerns back to a practical level. Some of the artists' comments about this process are reproduced as text here, as they were on the gallery wall.

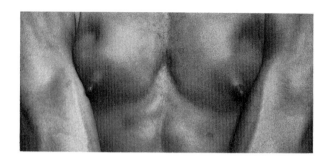

TRADITIONS AND REVERSALS

'The first hour I took some portrait shots, I could tell he was afraid of the request "please take off your clothes now".'

'Yes it's a man's body, so why do I feel so worried that I might objectify him. I actually stopped in the middle of a shoot.'

'They behave just like girls do . . . ecstatic to be a model, to have a chance to reveal themselves to the camera.'

'We laughed to begin with because it is so hackneyed, but then it became slow and serious. My mouth was really dry.'

'I was going to credit my printer but now he doesn't want his name associated with the show.'

'It's a theatre to experiment with raw emotions towards the male body; to worship it, fear it, use it for sex, play with it, attack it. Being vulgar and sincere at once.'

'At the moment when I felt he was most vulnerable, and I felt a bit invasive, he said that the intensity of concentration, lights, lens, and eye focused on his body made him feel secure.'

DIANE BAYLIS
And Then He Kissed Me
1992

DIANE BAYLIS
Abroad
1992

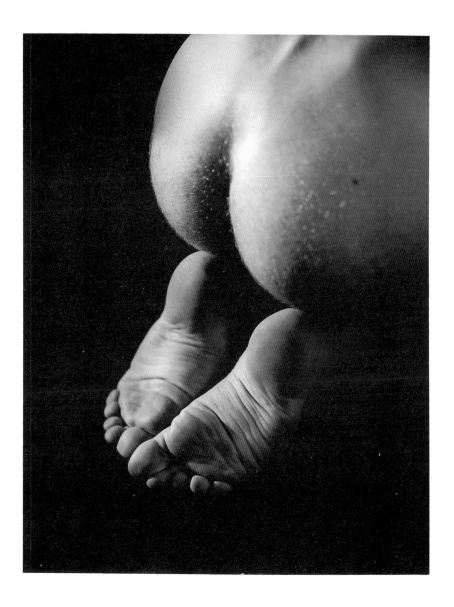

SARAH PUCILL
Untitled I
1993

BRIGITTE MARIA MAYER
David
1992

SUE LANZON
Untitled
1983

SUE EVANS
Venus De Milo
1992

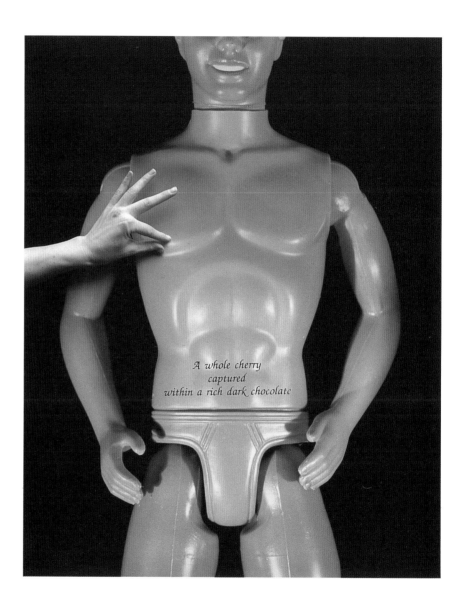

A whole cherry
captured
within a rich dark chocolate

EMMA WATERS
Untitled (Light Box)
1992

HONEY SALVADORI
Archaos
1992

**GUERRILLA GIRLS GO
BACK TO THE JUNGLE**

Since the socially responsible, multi-cultural
artworld of the 1990's has met the following
demands, Guerrilla Girls are pleased to announce
their retirement.

- All museums and galleries have publicly apologized for years of discrimination.
- The Far Right is undergoing psychoanalysis to determine the real source of its interest in Robert Mapplethorpe.
- Congress has legislated that sex is no longer obscene, but bailing out the Savings and Loan industry is.
- To fight art censorship, Sotheby's and Christie's have pledged 3% of their $5 billion annual sales to finance the N.E.A.'s $171 million budget.
- Guerrilla Girls have brokered the purchase of M.O.M.A. by a Japanese industrialist provided no more retrospectives be given to Frank Stella.
- *Artforum* has banned the following words: tough, virile, muscular, seminal, potent, genius, masterpiece, primitive and post-feminist.
- Leo Castelli, Mary Boone, Larry Gagosian, BlumHelman and Pace have endowed a foundation in our honor to eradicate chauvinism and racism in the artworld.

496 LaGuardia Pl. #237, NY 10012   **GUERRILLA GIRLS** ᵥ FORMER CONSCIENCE OF THE ARTWO

GUERILLA GIRLS
Artforum Project
1989

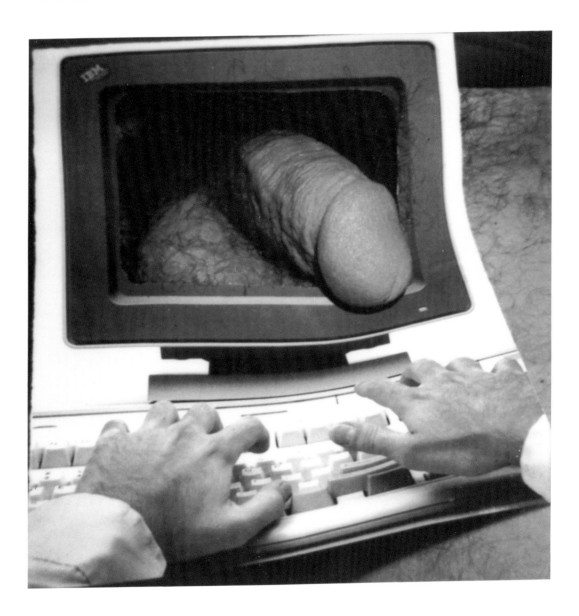

FLO FOX
User Friendly
1990

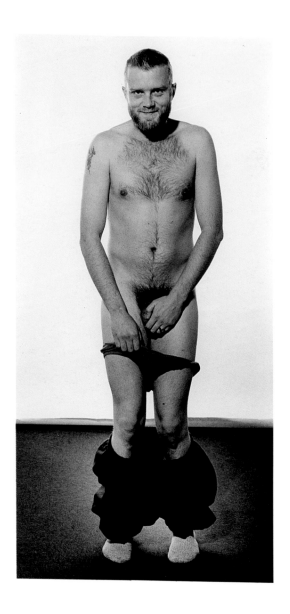

IONA FABIAN
Ivan
1992

Safer sex, they say, does not necessarily need to involve penetrative sex, but if it does then a condom should be worn. To be effective educationally, advertisements making this clear need to show naked men, possibly with erections, fitting or wearing condoms. So far in Britain such explicit illustrations have been banned.

LISA RIDING
Fully Exposed
1992

Divestment *(Substantives)*, nudity, denuding, denudation, stripping, uncovering, decortication, peeling, flaying, excoriation, desquamation, moulting, exfoliation.

(Adjectives) bare, naked, nude, stripped, denuded, undressed, unclothed, unclad, undraped, uncovered, unshod, barefoot, bareheaded, unbonneted, exposed, in dishabille.

(Verbs) To divest, uncover, denude, bare, strip, unclothe, undress, unrobe, disrobe, disapparel, debag, disarray, take off, doff, cast off, peel, pare, decorticate, husk, uncoif, unbonnet.

(Phrases) In a state of nature: stark-naked: *in puris naturalibus*: stripped to the buff: in one's birthday suit: bald as a coot: as bare as the back of one's hand.

LISA RIDING
Divestment
1992

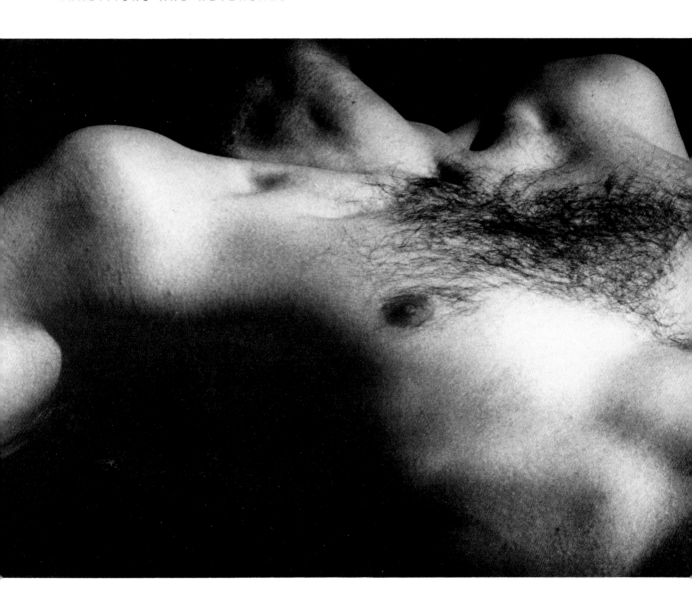

LOUISE CRAWFORD
Claiming Territory: The Male Torso
1992

TOVE KURTZWEIL
Close-up
1989

SUKI DHANDA
The Hands and Knee
1992

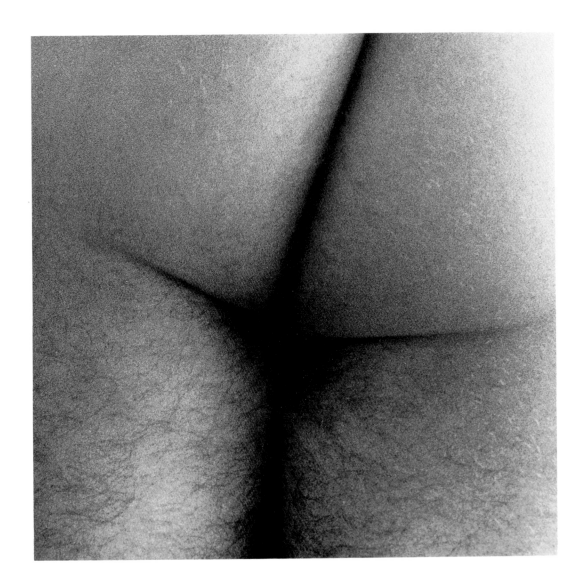

TOVE KURTZWEIL
Close-up
1989

MANGEL MANOVEL
Untitled
1989

TRISH MORRISSEY
Blue Body I
1992

TRISH MORRISSEY
Blue Body II
1992

SARA LEIGH LEWIS
George
1983

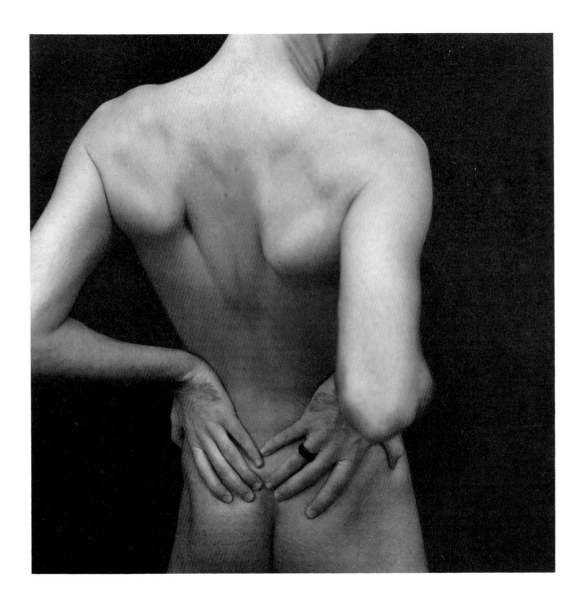

ANNE LEIGNIEL
Untitled
1988

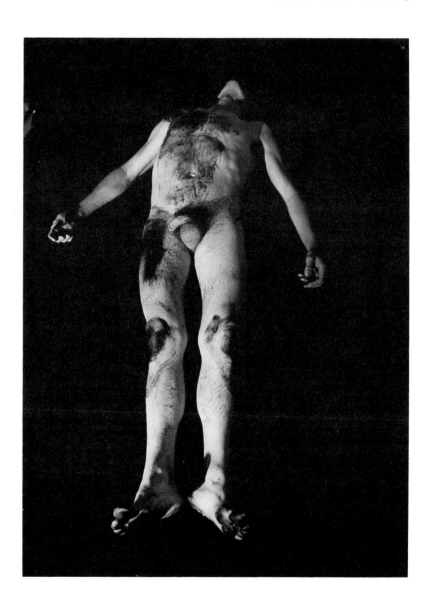

SARAH PUCILL
Untitled II
1993

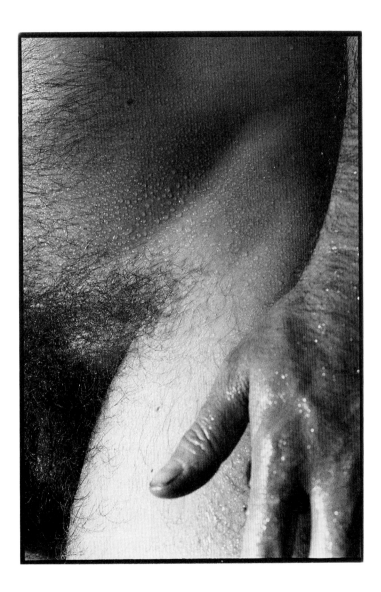

JACQUELINE KENNEDY
Advancing
1991

NADEGE MERIAU
Untitled
1992

LUCINDA BEATTY
What I Want is to Flow
1992

SUZANNE GREENSLADE
Double Crack
1984

SUE FOX
Buyaka
1991

DOMESTIC SCENES

'I've wanted to take this picture for years.'

'The first time we argued all night about everything and didn't go to bed until 6 a.m. I didn't take any pictures.'

'He was jealous because I was the one producing the work.'

'To begin with I was the more embarrassed one, even though I know him so well. He found it a turn-on . . . I was nervous that the light reading was wrong.'

'It made me feel immoral wanting to photograph him and leave him at once.'

'Oh and he didn't like me taking pictures of his dick when it was limp . . . "take a picture when it's big".'

'When I arranged him with the food, I became confused about whether the picture was to be appetising, for eating, or if I was doing a still life, which is very different. Is a man for nourishment or display?'

'I come into contact with this part of him when we lie together, when we get dressed, when he has a bath or a piss and I am there. To photograph it makes what I know into an image, maybe that is too available.'

SHANTA RAO
Masturbation 1
1992

SHANTA RAO
Le Fauteuil
1992

SHANTA RAO
Querelle
1992

YANNA PAPAIOANNOU
Headless
1992

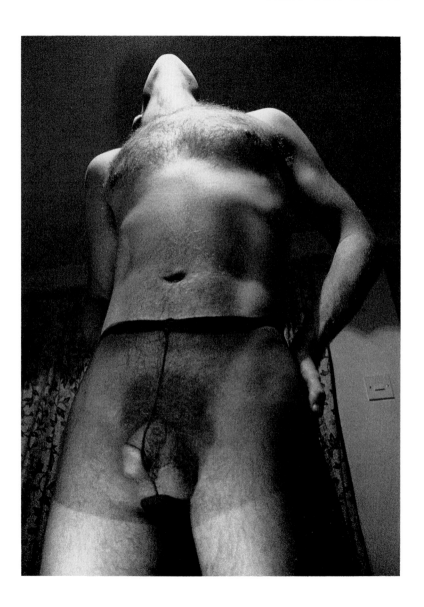

FIONA LORD
Man in Tights
1992

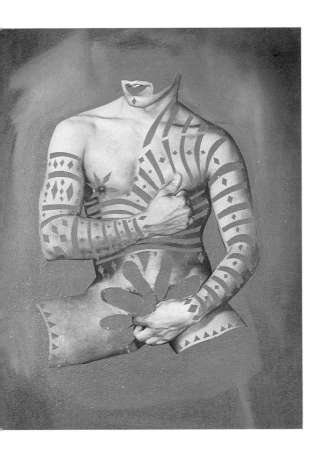

CATHY WARD
Play Jack Pudding
1992

CATHY WARD
Sunshine
1992

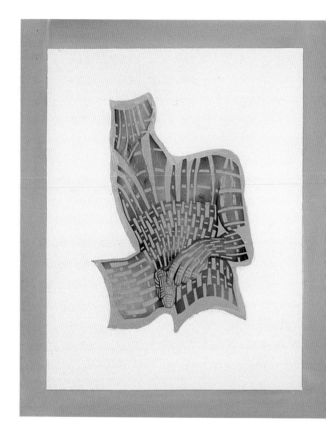

CATHY WARD
Pure
1992

CATHY WARD
Enmesh
1992

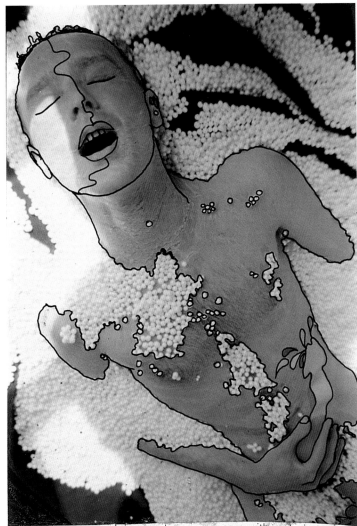

Tantra maintains that man can have an orgasm without losing semen

JUSTINE GARRATTY
Tantra Lover
1992

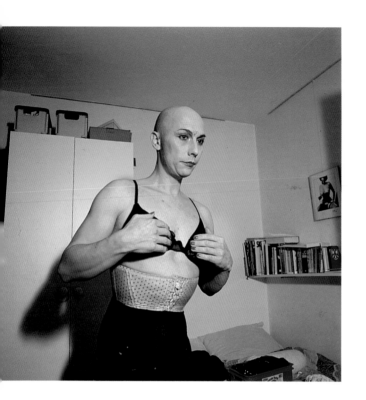

GRACE LAU
From 'Transformations'
1992

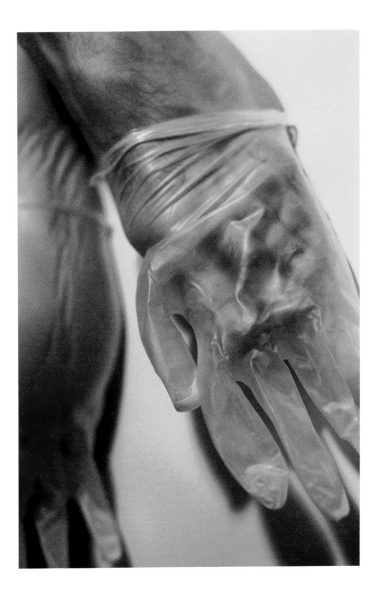

GRIEG MILES
Whatever Tickles Your Fancy
1990

YANNA PAPAIOANNOU
Overstep
1992

YANNA PAPAIOANNOU
The Audition
1992

TABITHA GOODE
Succulent I
1993

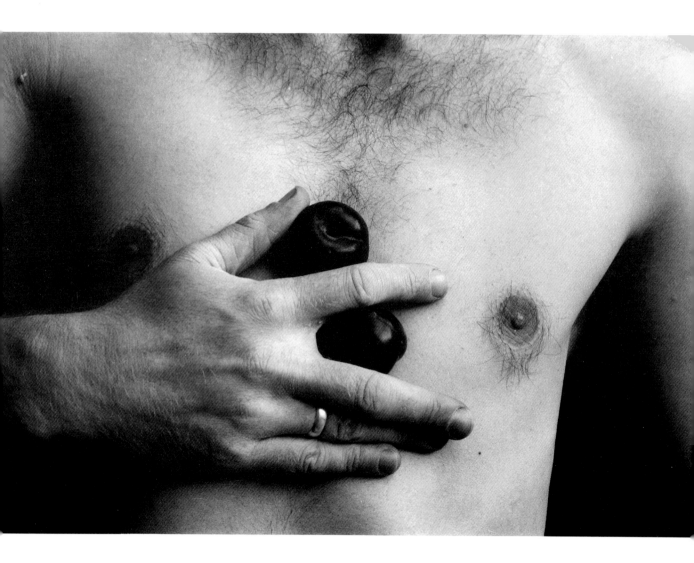

MARY PEYTON JONES
Ripe
1992

HARRIET THOMPSON
Paul, ex Lover
1990

HARRIET THOMPSON
Paul, ex Lover
1990

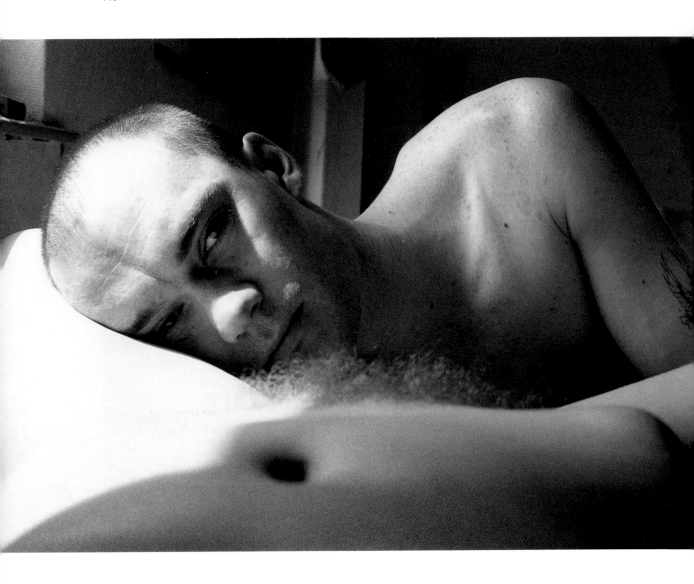

STEPHANIE VIDAL-HALL
Fressing
1993

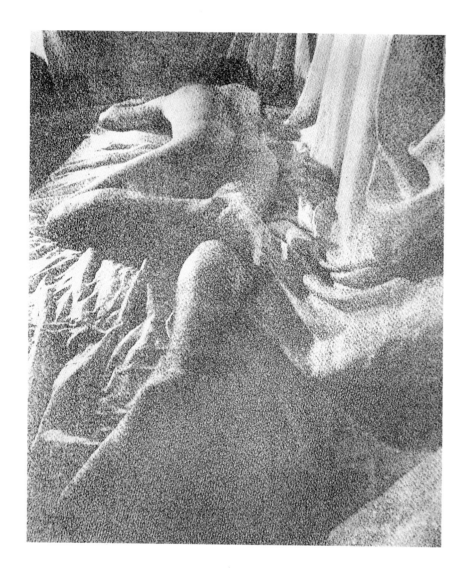

PERI ORHAN
David
1985

TERRYL BACON
Pan
1990

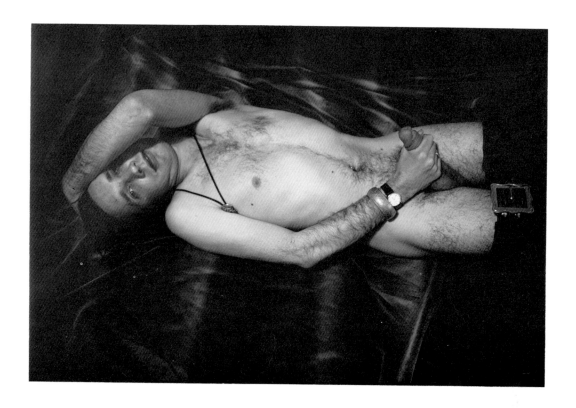

VANESSA JONES
Man Lying Masturbating
1992

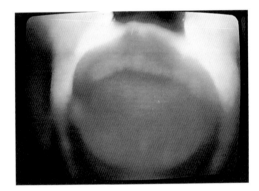

KATHARINE MEYNELL
Vampire Seat [Video Installation]
1992

SOPHIE MOLINS
The Sink
1992

UNKNOWN TERRITORIES

'When I first started taking pictures of his penis, I would get headaches.'

'We discussed the moment of orgasm and what happens to your body, like two scientists.'

'I look down through the view finder, I feel horny, I must be bad.'

'We don't know much about them, many probably know them more by touch than by sight.'

'A woman's body inside a man's body, the woman/eye/camera penetrating him.'

'Then there is worry of how to take these to a processing lab, and pick them up.'

'I was overwhelmed by an urge to reach my hand out and touch the body in the photograph; looking at it enacted a moment of my desire.'

'It's not all right for me to look at you, is it? But you find any excuse to display yourself to other men.'

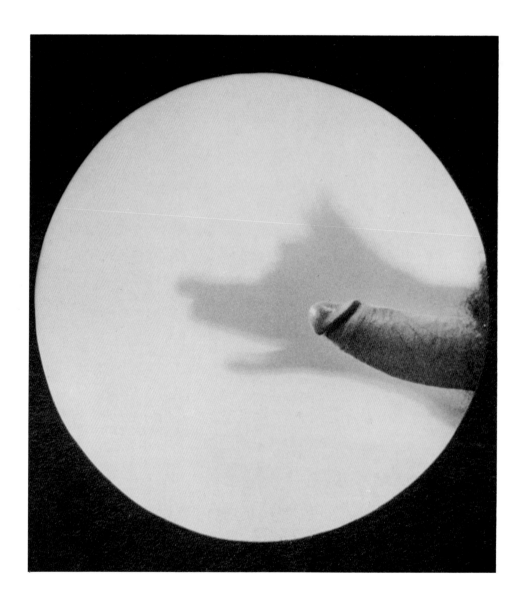

DIANE BAYLIS
Who's Afraid of the Big Bad Wolf?
1992

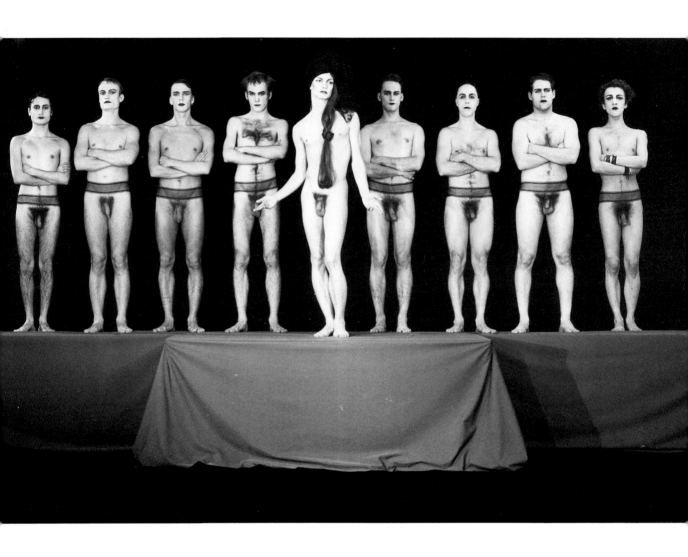

BRIGITTE MARIA MAYER
The Last Supper
1991

HERLINDE KOELBL
Cockerel Cock I
1984

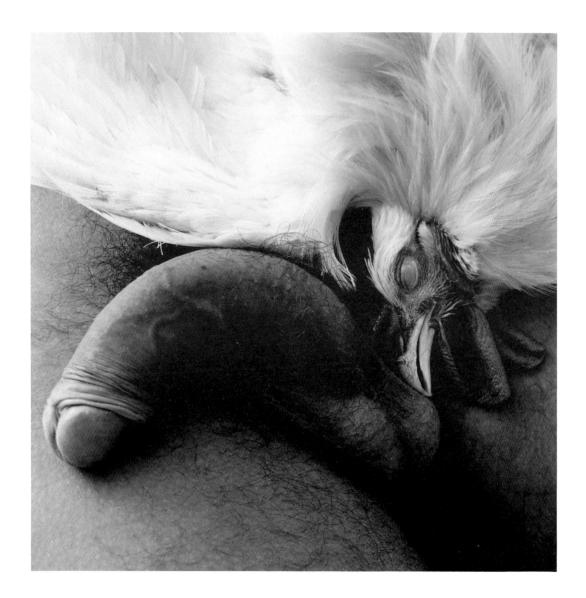

HERLINDE KOELBL
Cockerel Cock II
1984

ROBIN SHAW
Textures
1993

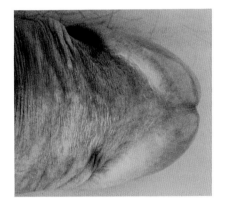

ROBIN SHAW
Textures
1993

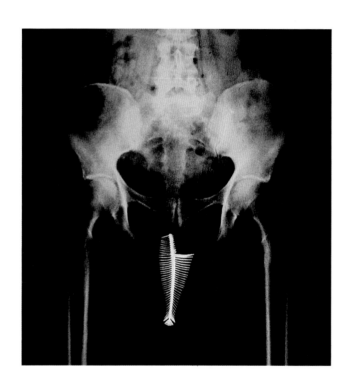
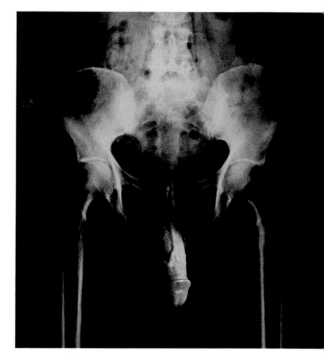

NAOMI SALAMAN
From 'Penis Envy'
1992

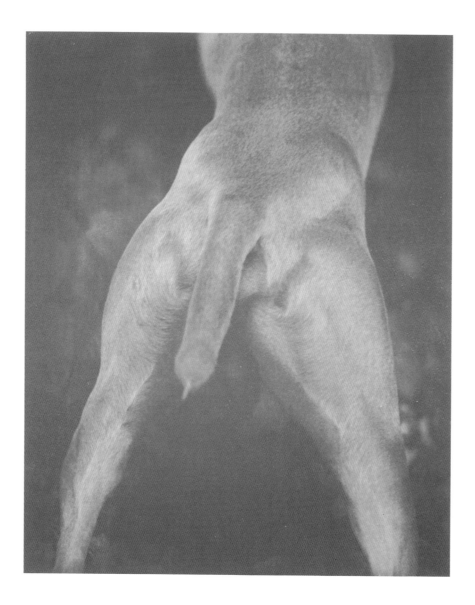

KAY HART
Sammy
1992

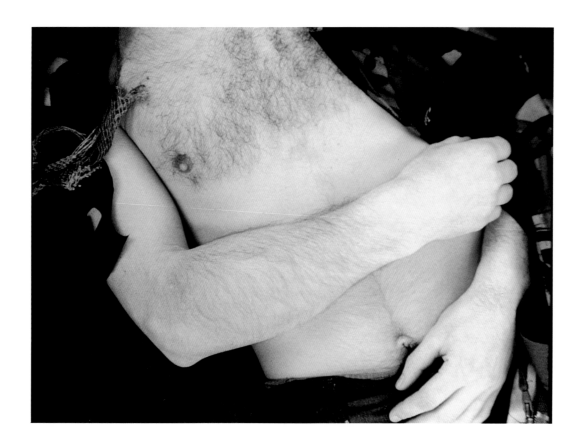

MOIRA McIVER
Subverted Expectations II
1992

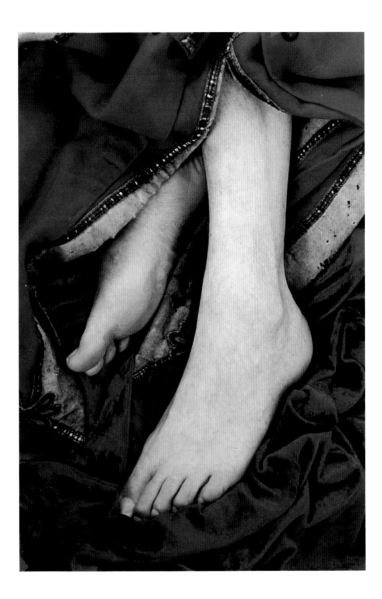

MOIRA McIVER
Seductive Myths I
1992

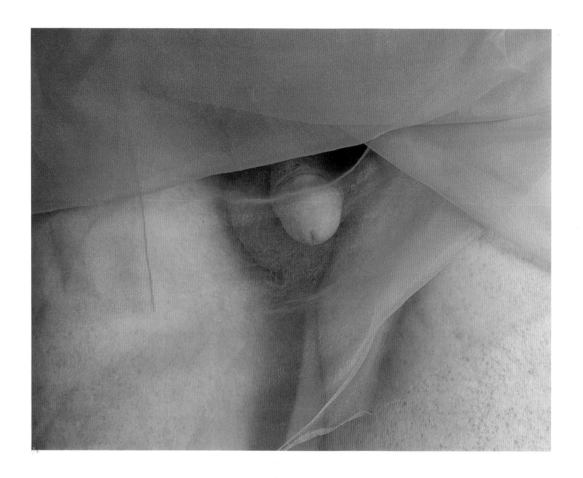

JANE RALLEY
Coq d'Azur (Stand Back and Let Go)
1991

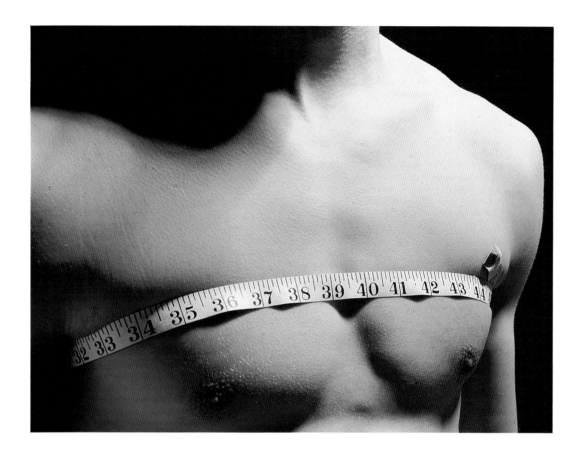

JANE ERSKINE
Vital Statistics
1992

HERMIONE WILTSHIRE
Still, Flying
1992

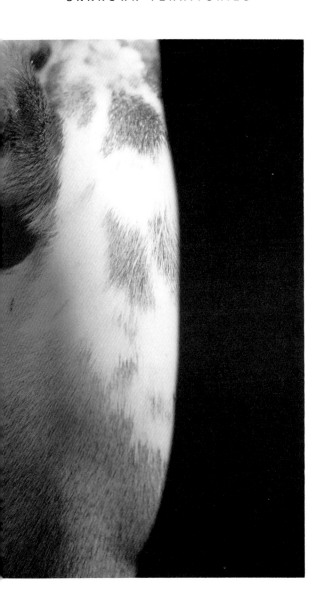

HERMIONE WILTSHIRE
Untitled
1993

JACQUELINE KENNEDY
Other Chambers
1991

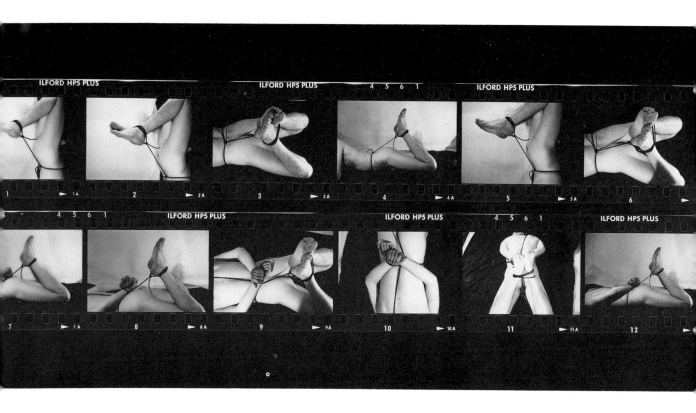

KAREN F
Untitled
1993

RUTH RUBINE
Liaison
1992

BRIGITTE MARIA MAYER
Auto Erotic Machine
1990

MARY PEYTON JONES
Put on Your Black Dress Baby
1992

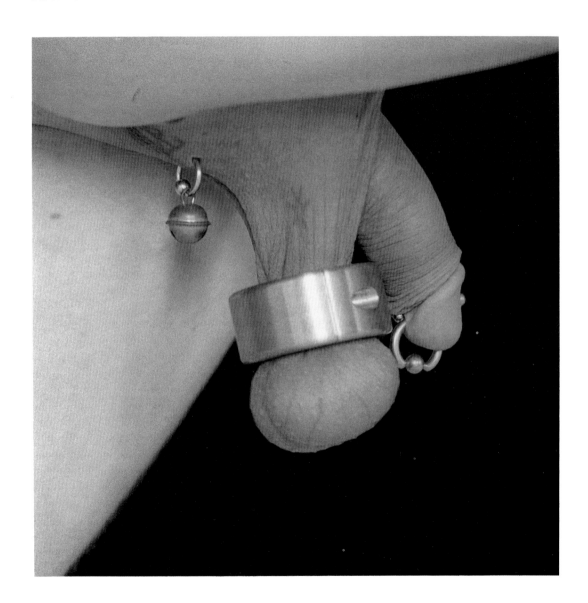

SALLY GRIFFYN
Adam's Secret
1992

LINDA CHAPMAN
Untitled
1992

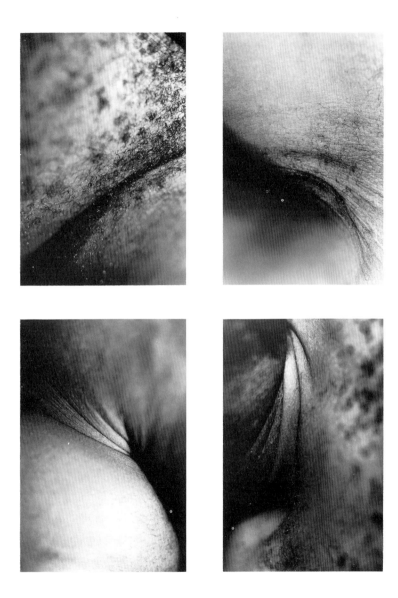

CHRIS DUYT
Untitled
1993

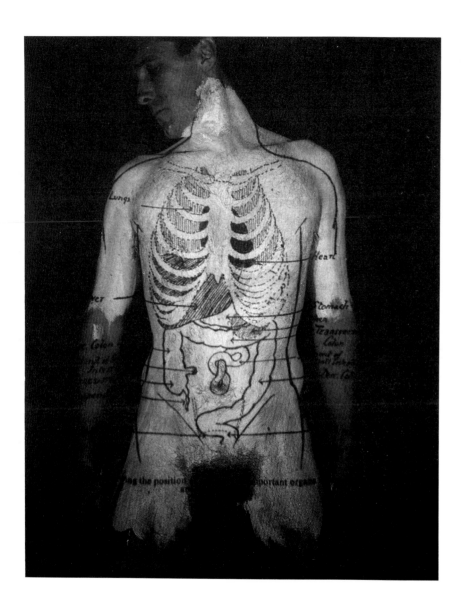

ANN ROGERS
Anatomy
1992

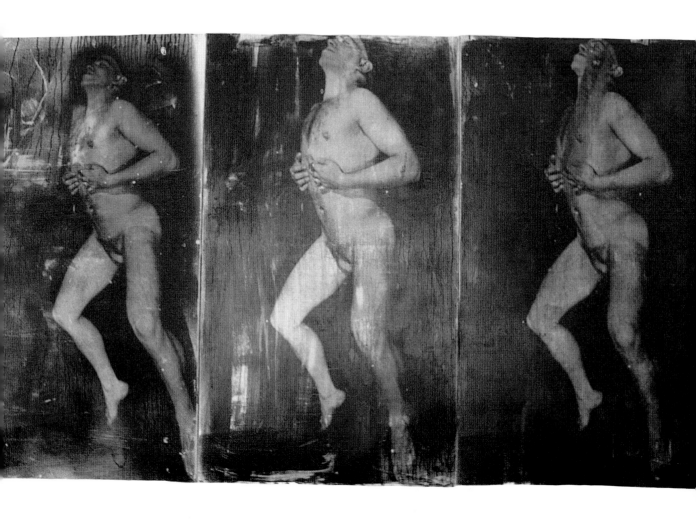

MARS GOMES
Franco
1992

KATHRYN EDWARDS
Rear
1992

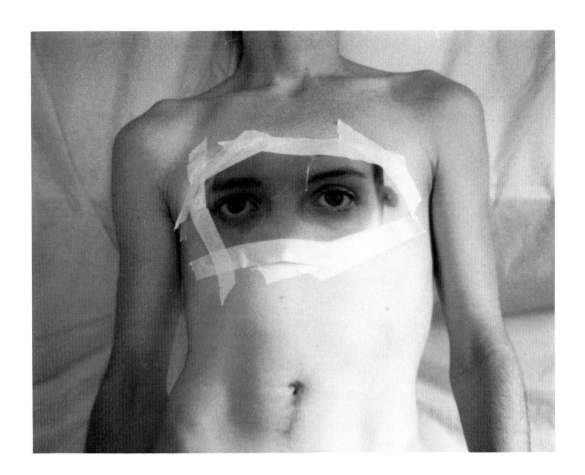

JENNIFER RYAN
Your You: Act 5
1992

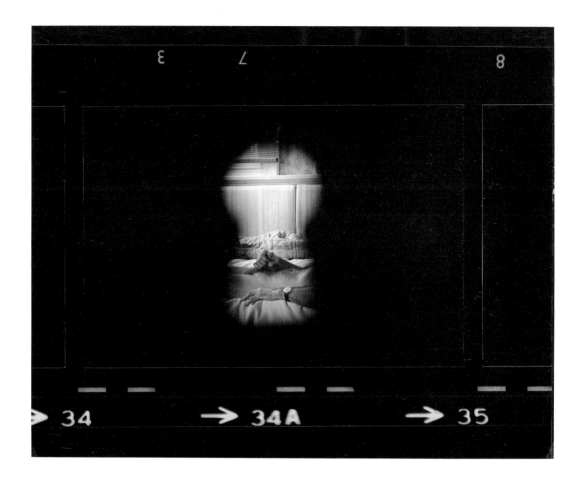

DIANE BAYLIS
In Bluebeard's Castle (detail)
1992

BIOGRAPHIES OF ARTISTS

TERRYL BACON   Born 1947, USA. Recent exhibitions: 1988, 'Friends', Bristol Colston Hall; 1989, 'Take Art', South West Arts, touring show; 1990, 'Evidence', Exeter University Reed Hall; 1993, 'Naked People', Brewhouse Theatre & Art Centre. Lecturer in photography. Lives in Somerset.

RUTH BATTEN   Born 1966, East London. Studied at University of Westminster. Freelance photographer, lives and works in London.

DIANE BAYLIS   Born 1943, Montreal, Canada. Studied Ecole De Beaux Arts, Montreal; Royal College of Art, London. Lives and works in Southern England.

LUCINDA BEATTY   Born 1958, Sussex. Studied Polytechnic of Central London. Recent exhibitions: 1988, Smith's of Covent Garden, London; 1988, Medici, London; 1990, Human Products, London. Portrait and commercial work. Lives and works in London.

SARA BYERS   Born 1966, Wiltshire. Studied sculpture, Camberwell School of Art; Royal College of Art, London. Recent exhibitions: 1987, 'Sogat '82 Exhibition', South London Art Gallery; 1987, 'Germinations IV', International touring group show; 1989, Art Directions Gallery, London; 1990, '4 Sculptors', Cheltenham College Gallery; 1992, Cheltenham Fellowship in Sculpture. Lives and works in London.

LINDA CHAPMAN   Born 1959, London. Studied at Open University. Recent exhibitions: 1991/92, London Salon; 1992/93, London Independent Photography. Freelance photographer, lives and works in London.

LOUISE CRAWFORD   Born 1961, Scotland. Studied Falmouth School of Art. Selected exhibitions: 1987, Smith Art Gallery & Museum, Stirling, Scotland; 1988, 'Marilyn, Modern Icon', Transmission Gallery, Glasgow; 1988, 'Intercom Festival', Bielefeld, Germany; 1989, Collective Gallery, Edinburgh; 1989, Oceaan Gallery, Arnhem, Holland; 1992, Transmission Gallery, Glasgow; 1992, 'Lux Europae', Light Project, Edinburgh. Artist/Film Maker, lives in Glasgow.

BARBARA DeGENEVIEVE   Born 1947, Pennsylvania, USA. Studied University New Mexico, Albuquerque. Selected group exhibition: 1992 'Flesh, Fetish, Fantasy', Film In The Cities, St Paul, Minnesota, USA; Selected solo exhibition: 1993, 'Between Thumb and Forefinger', Eye Gallery, San Francisco.

SUKI DHANDA   Born 1969, Berkshire. Studied photography, Plymouth College Art and Design. Recent exhibition: 1991, Smith's of Covent Garden, London. Freelance photographic assistant, lives and works in London.

CHRIS DUYT   Born 1957, Essex. Studied Goldsmiths College, London. Selected exhibitions: 1985, 'Image and Exploration', The Photographer's Gallery, London; 1987, 'The Ties That Bind: the family in contemporary art', The Collins Gallery, Glasgow. Lives and works in London.

KATHRYN EDWARDS   Born 1967, Wrexham, Wales. Studied at Maidstone College of Art. Selected exhibitions: 1991, 'Sign of the Times', Camerawork, London; 1992 'Rendez Vous', Maison de Faience, Desvre, France; 'She heard it on the radio', Watershed, Bristol; 1993 'Rendez Vous 2', Herbert Read Gallery, Canterbury. Lives and works in Kent.

JANE ERSKINE   Born 1972, Essex. Studied photography, West Surrey College of Art and Design. Recent exhibitions: 1991, 'Second Sight', The Photographers Gallery, London; 'First Exposure', Dixon Gallery, London. Lives and works in Surrey.

SUE EVANS   Born 1956, South Wales. 1988, set up 'ffoto fictions'. Recent exhibitions: 'South Glamorgan Artists', Chapter Arts Centre, Cardiff; 1989, 'Benson & Hedges Gold Awards', Hamiltons Gallery, London; 1990, 'Benson & Hedges Gold Awards', Mall Galleries, London; 1990, 'Probity of Virtue', Mostyn Art Gallery, Wales; 1991, 'Contact', Royal Festival Hall, London; 1992, 'Icon', Royal Festival Hall, London; Le Salon International de la Récherche Photographique de Royan, France; 1993, 'Permanent Waves', Central Library, Cardiff. Lives and works in Cardiff.

KAREN F   Selected exhibitions: 1988, 'Woman's Festival of Photography', Hope Street Gallery, Liverpool; 1991, 'Golden Nuggets', The Hanover Galleries, Liverpool; 1992, '83a opens', Bold Street, Liverpool; 1992, 'Lancashire Contemporaries', The Harris Museum, Preston; 1992, 'Karen F Exposes Herself', The Baa Baa, Liverpool; 1993, 'Visual Stress 1993', The Open Eye Gallery, Liverpool. Lives and works in Liverpool.

IONA FABIAN   Born 1968. Studied at Bath College of Higher Education. Lives and works in Yorkshire.

FLO FOX   Born 1945, Miami, Florida. Most recent exhibition: 1993, Duggal Downtown, New York City. Independent photographer, lives and works in New York.

SUE FOX   Born 1963. Studied teaching, Manchester Polytechnic. Selected exhibition: 1991. Solo show, The Pankhurst Centre, Manchester. Works and teaches in Manchester.

JUSTINE GARRATTY   Born 1964. Studied Brighton Polytechnic. Selected exhibition: 1992, 'Seasonally Adjusted Figures', The Muse Gallery, Brighton. Lives and works in Sheffield.

MARS GOMES   Born 1959, Beira, Mozambique. Studied at Instituto Portugues de Fotografia, Lisbon; Canterbury College of Art, Kent Institute of Art and Design; Central St. Martins College of Art, London. Selected shows: 1986, Lesbian and Gay Show, Brixton Art Gallery, London; 1990, 'The Cornfield', Syracuse University, USA; 1991, 'Puff', Zeppelin Studios, Amsterdam; 1993, 'Independent Artists on the Market', Brixton, London. Lives and works in London.

TABITHA GOODE   Born 1968, Hertfordshire. Studied at University of East London; currently studying at University of Westminster. Selected exhibitions: 1991, 'The Bottom Drawer', Acton Community Arts Workshop. Lives and works in London.

JULIE GORHAM   Born 1971, Suffolk. Studied at West Surrey College of Art and Design, Farnham.

SUZANNE GREENSLADE   Born 1952, Georgia, USA. Studied at Tulane University and Southeastern Center for the Arts, Atlanta, Georgia. Lecturer in Photography, Swansea and Cardiff. Selected exhibitions: 1982, 'Clisonné and Clouds', Front Street Gallery, North Carolina; 1991, 'Pivot', Oriel Mostyn, South Wales. Lives and works in Wales.

SALLY GRIFFYN   Born 1962, Bridlington, North Yorkshire. Studied at University of Toronto, Canada; University of Westminster, London. Freelance photographer.

GUERILLA GIRLS   Anonymous group of women artists, formed in the early 1980s in New York.

KAY HART   Born 1962, Nottingham. Studied University of Westminster, London.

Selected shows: 1989, 'Grolsch New Talent', Café de Paris, London; 1992, 'Icon', South Bank Photo Show, London; 1992, Solo show, Metro Cinema, London. Freelance photographer, lives in London.

VANESSA JONES   Born 1966, Northampton. Studied at Leeds Polytechnic; University of Westminster. Recent exhibition: 1992, 'Women Photographers', Blackfriars Photography Project. Lives and studies in London.

JACQUELINE KENNEDY   Born 1949, London. Selected exhibitions: 1987, Painting, The London Group, Royal College of Art; 1988, Video/Painting in Progress, The Imperial War Museum; 1991, Photography, Portfolio Gallery, London; 1992, Photography, Norwich Arts Centre. Lives and works in London.

HERLINDE KOELBL   Born 1949, Lindau, Germany. Selected solo exhibitions: 1990, Museum Für Kunst und Gewerbe, Hamburg; 1990, Historisches Museum, Vienna; 1991, Spertus Museum, Chicago; 1992, Heidi Reckermann Gallery, Cologne; 1992, Palais Palffy, Vienna; 1992 Staatliche Galerie, Moritzburg Halle; 1992, Charach Epstein Museum Gallery, Detroit; 1993, Images Gallery, Cincinnati. Selected group exhibition: 'Behold the Man', The Photographer's Gallery, 1987, London. Lives and works in Munich.

TOVE KURTZWEIL   Born 1938, Denmark. Founded Tegn Foto/Tegn Photo. Selected exhibitions: 1988, 'Form', The Royal Danish Academy, Copenhagen; 1989, 'Erotic', Overgarden, The Exhibition Hall, The Ministry of Culture, Copenhagen; 1992, Tove Kurtzweil, '25 Years of Portraits', Gallery Photographica, Copenhagen; 1992, 'Souvenirs', Lund Photographic Gallery, Lund; 1992, 'Marks After Meetings II', Kvinfo, Copenhagen; 1993, 'Egypt', Krasnapolsky, Copenhagen; 1993, 'Intimate Pictures', Lund Photographic Gallery, Lund. Lives and works in Copenhagen.

SUE LANZON   Born in Taiping, Malaya, 1955. Studied photography at Bournemouth Illustrator. Selected exhibitions: 1983, 'Best Boys', Janapa Gallery, New York; 1986, 'Song of the Ruined Innocent', Garden Gallery, London; 1987, 'Benson & Hedges Gold Awards', Hamiltons Gallery, London; 1990, Visage Gallery, London. Lives and works in London.

GRACE LAU   Born 1940, London. Studied at University of Westminster, London; Newport College of Documentary Photography. Founded 'Exposures', 1992. Selected exhibitions: 1987, 'Photo Exposures', Submarine Gallery, London; 1992, Larmes d'Eros Gallery, Paris. Lives and works in London.

SARA LEIGH LEWIS   Born 1957, Bristol. Studied at John Cass School of Art, London. Lives and works in London.

ANNE LEIGNIEL   Born 1963, France. Studied at the National School of Art, Paris; London College of Printing. Selected exhibitions: 1988, Le Baglama, Paris; 1989, FIAPAD,

Paris; 1990, Royal Photographic Society, London; 1991/1992, Portfolio Gallery, London; 1992, Manley's Gallery, London. Photographer, lives and works in London.

FIONA LORD   Born 1965. Studied Central St. Martins School of Art; Pimlico Arts and Media. Freelance photographer, works and lives in London.

MANGEL MANOVEL   Born 1962, Spain. Studied West Surrey College of Art and Design, Farnham. Selected exhibitions: 1988, 'Flesh', Watershed Media Centre, Bristol; 1989, 'Chains and Flesh', Colston Hall Art Gallery, Bristol.

BRIGITTE MARIA MAYER   Born Regensburg, Germany, 1965. Selected exhibitions: 1987, 'Documenta 8', Sektor 29 Gallery, Kassell; 1990, 'Lust and Pornography, Pornography and Lust', Berlin; 1992, Loulou Lassard Gallery, Berlin. Independent photographer, lives and works in Berlin.

MOIRA MCIVER   Born 1962, Scotland. Studied National College of Art and Design, Dublin; University of Ulster, Belfast. Selected exhibitions: 1987, 'Identities', Art and research exchange, Belfast; 1991, 'New Irish Realities', The Ash Gallery, Edinburgh; 1992, 'Men in Uniform', The Oliver Dowling Gallery, Dublin. Lives and works in Belfast.

NADEGE MERIAU   Born in France. Currently studying at Bournemouth College of Art.

KATHARINE MEYNELL   Born 1954, London. Studied at Royal College of Art, London. Selected exhibitions: 1988, 'Bookworks', Victoria and Albert Museum, London; 1989 'Video Wall', Tate Gallery, Liverpool; 'Femme Cathodique', Palais de Tokyo, Paris; Installation, Cornerhouse, Manchester; 'Acts of Remembrance', Harris Museum, Preston; 1990, 'Book Works', British Museum Library; 1992, International Centre of Photography, New York, 'Video Eat' and 'Vampire Seat', Installation at Kettles Yard, Cambridge; 1992, 'Pullit X', Pullit, London; Women's Art at New Hall, Cambridge.

GRIEG MILES   Born 1963, Nottingham. Studied at Newcastle Polytechnic. Lives and works in London.

SOPHIE MOLINS   Born 1964, London. Studied at Chelsea College of Art; Derby College of Higher Education; Maryland Institute of Art. Selected exhibitions: 1991, 'Treading a Fine Line', Zelda Cheatle, London; 1992, South Bank Open Photography Exhibition, London; 1992, Two Woman Show, The Special Photographer's Company, London; 1992, Metro Cinema, London. Lives and works in London.

TRISH MORRISSEY   Born 1967, Dublin. Studied at College of Technology, Dublin. Selected exhibitions: 1987, 'Dublin, a City Destroyed', Trinity College, Dublin; 1991/1992, Fuji/Association of Photographers' Assistants Award Exhibition, Association's Gallery, London; 1993, 'Silent Voices', Baptists' School, Leeds; 'Six of the Best', Vic Naylor's,

London; 'Couples', The Hales Gallery, London. Freelance photographer, lives and works in London.

PERI ORHAN   Born 1962, London. Currently studying photography at Brighton West University.

IOANNA PAPAIOANNOU   Born 1968, Athens. Studied at Brighton Polytechnic. Artist, dancer and choreographer, lives and works in London.

MARY PEYTON JONES   Born 1957, Plymouth. Studied at Bradford University. Works as a costumier, lives in London.

SARAH PUCILL   Born 1961, Amersham. Studied at Crewe; Slade School of Art; East London University. Recent exhibitions: 1990, 'New Contemporaries', ICA, London; 'Against the Grain', Camera Work, London; 1991, Graduate Group Show, Sandra Higgins, London; 'Woman in my Life', Acton Community Arts, London; 'Archaeology of Silence', Finsbury Park, London; 1992, 'North West Open', Corner House, Manchester; 1993, 'West Open', Riverside Studios, London. Film-maker and photographer, lives and works in London.

JANE RALLEY   Born 1957, Luton. Studied at Leeds University; London College of Printing; Regent's College. Selected exhibitions: 1986, Soho Poly Gallery, London; 1992, 'Stand Back and Let Go', Freud Café Gallery, London. Lives and works in London.

IZZI RAMSEY   Born 1948, London. Studied at University of Westminster. Selected exhibition: 1992, Pleasures of the Senses, Carnaby Street, London. Freelance photographer and teacher, lives and works in London.

SHANTA RAO   Born 1966, Lille, France. Selected exhibitions: 1991, 'Women of South India'; 1992, 'Women of Mauritania', Arab World Institute, Paris; 1993, 'Mauritania: Gesture and Matter', Chelles, France. Lives and works in Paris.

LISA RIDING   Born 1968, Castleford, West Yorkshire. Studied at Bretton Hall College, University of Leeds. Selected exhibitions: 1992, 'New Designers', Business Design Centre, London; 1993, 'Wombat', Elizabeth Gallery, Wakefield. Lives and works in Newcastle upon Tyne.

ANN ROGERS   Born 1955, Leicester. Studied at University of Middlesex. Selected exhibitions: 1991, 'Cornucopia', Smiths Gallery, London; 1991, 'The Face', Prema Gallery, London; 1991, 'An Angel in My Basement', Special Photographers, London; 1991, 'South Bank Photo Show', Royal Festival Hall, London; 1992, 'Fusion', Photofusion, London; 1992, 'Beyond the Portrait', Derby Photography Festival. Lives and works in London.

RUTH RUBINE   Born 1960, Austria. Recent exhibition: 1990, 'Paganism', Young Unknowns Gallery, London. Portrait photographer, lives and works in London.

JENNIFER RYAN   Born 1971, Scotland. Currently studying at Glasgow School of Art. Selected show: 1991, Newbury Gallery, Glasgow.

NAOMI SALAMAN   Born 1963, Cambridge. Studied at Chelsea School of Art; Derby University. Selected exhibitions: 1988, 'The Invisible Man', Goldsmith's Gallery, London; 1990, 'Post Morality' Kettle's Yard, Cambridge; 1991, 'Sign of the Times', Camerawork, London; 1992, 'Penis Envy', Metro Cinema, London. Lives and works in London.

HONEY SALVADORI   Born 1958, London. Studied at Middlesex University. Freelance photographer, London.

ROBIN SHAW   Born 1961, New York. Studied Middlesex Polytechnic; Derby University. Recent exhibitions: 1990, 'Danger Zones', Camerawork, London; 'Post Morality', Kettles Yard, Cambridge; 1991, 'The Male Nude', Portfolio Gallery, London; 1992, 'Addressing The Forbidden', Stills Gallery, Edinburgh. Lives and works in London.

CHARLOTTE SMITH   Born 1964. Studied at Nottingham Polytechnic. Selected exhibitions: 1990, 'A Dozen Ways', Bonnington Gallery, Nottingham; 1992, 'Material', Ikon, Birmingham. Lives and works in London.

HARRIET THOMPSON   Born 1962, High Wycombe. Studied at Manchester Polytechnic. Selected exhibitions: 1990, Photos accepted at Oxford Museum of Modern Art and at Young Unknowns Gallery, London; 1991, Corner House Bar, Manchester. Lives and works in Manchester.

STEPHANIE VIDAL-HALL   Born 1968. Studied at Nottingham Trent University. Lecturer at Nottingham Trent University. Lives and works in Nottingham.

SIW WAAGE   Born 1963, Molde, Norway. Studied at Blinden University, Oslo; Middlesex University. Selected exhibitions: 1988, Goethe Institut, Oslo; 1992, Paintings, 'Gallery', Molde, Norway. Lives and works in London.

CATHY WARD   Born 1960, Kent. Studied Middlesex Polytechnic; Royal College of Art, London. Selected exhibitions: 1988 'Metamorphoses', Camden Galleries, London; 1988, 'Wet', Smith's Gallery, London; 1989, 'Key', Walter Phillips Gallery, Alberta, Canada; 1990, 'Sperm Bank' (installation), New York; 1991, 'The Beauty Boxes', Alternative Art Galleries, London; 1992, 'Assumed Identities', Metro Cinema, London; 1992, 'Pullitt X', Pullitt, Camden, London. Lives and works in London.

EMMA WATERS   Born 1966, Reading. Studied at Polytechnic South West, Exeter.

Selected exhibitions: 1988, 'Pins and Needles', Polytechnic South West, Exeter; 1989, 'Out of Bounds', City Studios, Exeter; 1990, 'Women in Art', Exeter Arts Centre; 'Artists with Ambition', Totnes Community Centre. Lives and works in London.

HERMIONE WILTSHIRE   Born 1963, London. Studied at Central School of Art and Design; Chelsea School of Art. Selected exhibitions: 1987, 'New British Art Show', Air Gallery, London; 1987, 'Name No Body', Riverside Studios, London; 1990, 'The Artist Selects', Goldsmith's Gallery, London; 1991, Riverside Studios, London; 1992, Lisson Gallery, London; 1992, 'Traces of the Figure', Stoke on Trent City Museum and Gallery. Lives and works in London.

LINDA CHRISTINE WHITE   Born 1972, County Durham. Studied at Cleveland College of Art. Lives and works in County Durham.

For further information on the artists and the exhibition, contact

The Women's Art Library
Fulham Palace
Bishops Avenue
London SW6 6EA
Telephone 081 731 7618

LIST OF ILLUSTRATIONS